AMERICAN IMPERIALISM
Viewpoints of United States
Foreign Policy, 1898-1941

Reproduced with the cooperation of the
Hoover Institution of War, Revolution and Peace,
Stanford University, Stanford, California

THE PANAMA CANAL

A Study in International Law and Diplomacy

Harmodio Arias

ARNO PRESS & THE NEW YORK TIMES

New York ★ 1970

Collection Created and Selected
by
CHARLES GREGG OF GREGG PRESS

Reprinted from a copy in The New York Public Library

Library of Congress Catalog Card Number: 79-111707
ISBN 0-405-02001-5

ISBN for complete set: 0-405-02000-7

Reprint Edition 1970 by Arno Press Inc.
Manufactured in the United States of America

STUDIES IN ECONOMICS AND POLITICAL SCIENCE.

Edited by HON. W. PEMBER REEVES,

Director of the London School of Economics and Political Science.

No. 25 in the Series of Monographs by Writers connected
with the London School of Economics and Political Science.

THE PANAMA CANAL

THE
PANAMA CANAL

A STUDY IN INTERNATIONAL LAW AND DIPLOMACY

BY

HARMODIO ARIAS, B.A., LL.B.

SOMETIME EXHIBITIONER AND PRIZEMAN OF ST. JOHN'S COLLEGE,
CAMBRIDGE
QUAIN PRIZEMAN IN INTERNATIONAL LAW, UNIVERSITY OF LONDON

LONDON
P. S. KING AND SON
ORCHARD HOUSE, WESTMINSTER
1911

PREFACE

ALL the maritime nations have interests of transcendent value on those sea-routes which, on account of their position as supplying the most convenient means of communication, may properly be called international. This is the reason why the civilised world has concentrated so much attention upon the question of the Panama Canal. The engineer has by now very nearly completed his share in the great task of uniting the Atlantic and the Pacific Oceans by means of a canal, thus providing a more rapid and easy means of intercourse between different peoples. It remains for the jurist to ascertain what is the legal position of the canal, so that this work of civilisation, being placed under the rule of law and justice, may be as productive of welfare to mankind as it is possible. It is his duty to examine the value of the international agreements that refer to the question of interoceanic transit under the light of legal theory and as resting on the hard facts of history, gauging at the same time the immediate effects not less than the possible consequences that may result from the adopted solution of the problem. In my endeavours to find the answer to the question relating to the legal status of the Panama Canal, it has been my aim to put aside any personal bias or national prejudice, thus endeavouring to carry into my work a judicial impartiality.

It seemed advisable, before dealing with the purely legal aspect of the question, to examine at some length the diplomatic history of the interoceanic transit, for such an inquiry would serve as a preliminary to the solution of the problem, thus placing us in a position to ascertain how far the status of the waterway is the result of a kind of compromise springing from the divers and conflicting interests and aspirations of the powers more directly affected by the opening of the new route. I have, therefore, dealt with the attitude of the United States towards the canal question, showing the variations that their policy in this connection has undergone in the course of years, and tracing the influence that Great Britain has brought to bear on this important problem. I have also discussed, somewhat briefly, the later amplifications of President Monroe's well-known message in their bearing on isthmian transit in the New World, thus reviewing the diplomatic wrangles that have resulted from the attempt of the United States to apply to this question their famous Doctrine in its advanced form.

In endeavouring to ascertain the position of the Panama Canal under the law of nations, I have not confined myself to the consideration of the treaty stipulations that exist with regard to the interoceanic communication. For in order to arrive at the solution of some international problems it is sometimes necessary to inquire into the requirements of life, without losing sight of the tendencies of the law as manifested in the modern intercourse of nations. International Law, it must be borne in mind, is inseparably intertwined with some other branches of social science. It is for this reason that many of the notions therein contained cannot be expounded satisfactorily by mere legal reasoning. I have also, therefore, briefly dealt with some important factors— such as the geographical position of the canal and the interest that all nations have on the question of transit— which undoubtedly throw much light on the ultimate position that the Panama Canal will be made to assume. From this, as well as from the purely legal standpoint, I have endeavoured to deal with the nature, causes, and consequences of the notion of neutralisation as applicable to waterways, and have also compared the Suez and Panama Canals in respect of their legal position, owing, especially, to the fact that the Hay-Pauncefote treaty, which purports to bestow on the Panama Canal the privileges and liabilities of neutralisation, avowedly adopts the Suez Convention as its model. I have concluded my little work by dealing briefly with the question as to whether the erection of fortifications on the route would be repugnant to the notion of neutralisation. An appendix has been provided with the purpose of supplying an easy means of reference to the different articles of the treaties that deal with the matter under consideration.

For the preparation of this essay it was found necessary to study a considerable number of state documents, general treatises on International Law, pamphlets, and monographs.

I have endeavoured throughout to acknowledge all the works from which I have derived assistance, hoping that this method, though cumbrous because it overloads the pages with too numerous references, may serve as a ready guide to those who may require a more detailed information, and also afford an opportunity for checking or correcting my assertions. The help that I have derived from Dr. A. Pearce Higgins, Lecturer in International Law at the London School of Economics, is of a different nature. I must acknowledge here my debt of gratitude towards him for his sympathetic aid in reading the whole of my manuscript, which has thus necessarily profited by his great care and profound judgment.

HARMODIO ARIAS.

THE LONDON SCHOOL OF ECONOMICS
AND POLITICAL SCIENCE,
May 16*th*, 1911.

CONTENTS

ix

LIST OF BOOKS AND ARTICLES QUOTED OR OTHERWISE RE-FERRED TO IN THE TEXT.

J. M. ABRIBAT, *Le Détroit de Magellan au point de vue international* (Paris, 1902).

A. ALVAREZ, "Histoire diplomatique des Républiques américaines et la Conférence de Mexico," *Revue général de droit international public*, tome ix.

Annals of The American Academy of Political and Social Science, July, 1903.

D. ANTOKOLETZ, *La doctrine de Monroë et l'Amérique latine* (Paris, 1905).

JOHN AUSTIN, *Lectures on Jurisprudence or the Philosophy of Positive Law* (London, 1904).

HENRY BONFILS, *Manuel de droit international public.* Cinquième édition. Par Paul Fauchille (Paris, 1908).

SIR CYPRIAN BRIDGE, "Naval Strategy and the Panama Canal," article in *The Times* (South American Supplement), November 29, 1910.

P. BUNAU-VARILLA, "La question de Panama," article in *La Nouvelle Revue*, April 15, 1904.

CHARLES CALVO, *Le Droit international théorique et pratique.* Cinquième édition, 1887–95.

CANAL DE PANAMÁ, *Documentos relacionados con este asunto que se publican por orden del Senado de la República* (Bogotá, Imprenta nacional, 1903).

George W. Davis, "Fortifications at Panama," in the *American Journal of International Law*, vol. iii.

De Bustamante, "Le canal de Panama et le droit international," *Revue de droit international et de legislation comparée*, tome xxvii.

Delarüe de Beaumarchais, *La doctrine de Monroë* (Paris, 1897).

Baron E. Descamps, *La neutralité de la Belgique au point de vue historique, diplomatique, juridique et politique* (Bruxelles, Paris, 1902).

Diplomatic Correspondence of the United States.

Foreign Relations of the United States.

M. García-Mérou, *Historia de la diplomacia americana—Política internacional de los Estados Unidos* (Buenos Aires, 1904).

F. Hagerup, *La neutralité permanente* (Paris, 1905).

Peter C. Hains, "The Neutralisation of the Panama Canal," in *The American Journal of International Law*, vol. iii.

J. B. Henderson, *American Diplomatic Questions* (New York, 1901).

A. Pearce Higgins, *The Hague Peace Conferences* (Cambridge, 1909).

T. E. Holland, *Studies in International Law* (Oxford, 1898).

G. F. W. Holls, *The Peace Conference at the Hague and its bearing on International Law and Policy* (New York, 1900).

C. H. Huberich, *The Trans-Isthmian Canal* (Austin, Texas, 1904).

L. M. Keasbey, *The Nicaragua Canal and the Monroe Doctrine* (New York, 1896).

H. S. Knapp, "The Real Status of the Panama Canal as regards Neutralisation," in *The American Journal of International Law*, vol. iv.

JOHN H. LATANÉ, *Diplomatic Relations of the United States and Spanish America* (Baltimore, 1900); "The Neutralisation Features of the Hay-Pauncefote Treaty," in the *Annual Report of the American Historical Association*, 1902.

T. J. LAWRENCE, *Principles of International Law*, 4th edition (London, 1910); *Essays on International Law.*

F. DE MARTENS, "La neutralisation du Danemark," in *La Revue des Deux Mondes*, November 15, 1903.

Messages and Papers of the Presidents of the United States.

A. MÉRIGNHAC, "La doctrine de Monroë à la fin du xixᵉ siècle," in *La Revue du droit public*, Mars–Avril, 1896.

JOHN BASSETT MOORE, *A Digest of International Law*, 1906.

M. MOYE, "L'imperialisme américain et la doctrine de Monroë," in *La Revue général de droit international public*, tome xii.

New York Herald, September 10, 1903.

L. OPPENHEIM, *International Law* (London, 1905).

Parliamentary Papers, 1901 (Cd. 438).

J. M. QUIJANO OTERO, *Informe sobre el Canal de Panamá* (Bogotá, 1875).

L. M. ROSSIGNOL, *Le Canal de Suez* (Paris, 1898).

A. ROUGIER, "La République de Panama," in *La Revue général de droit international public*, tome xii.

G. H. SULLIVAN AND W. N. CROMWELL, *Compilation of Executive Documents and Diplomatic Correspondence relative to a Trans-Isthmian Canal in Central America* (New York, 1903).

J. B. SCOTT, "The United States and Latin America," *The Times*, (South American Supplement), November 29, 1910.

J. T. SULLIVAN, *Report of Historical and Technical Information relating to the Problem of Interoceanic Communication by way of the American Isthmus*, 1883.

The Times, June 1, 1910, and November 29, 1910 (South American Supplement).

I. D. Travis, *The History of the Clayton-Bulwer Treaty*, 1900.

A. Viallate, *Essais d'histoire diplomatique américaine* (Paris, 1905).

John Westlake, *International Law*, Part I. (Cambridge, 1904).

Wharton, *Digest of International Law of the United States.*

Wheaton, *Elements of International Law*, Dana's edition.

J. G. Whiteley, "Les traités Clayton-Bulwer et Hay-Pauncefote," in *La Revue général de droit international public*, tome iii., 2ᵉ série.

T. S. Woolsey, "Suez and Panama—A Parallel," in *Annual Report of the American Historical Association*, 1902.

THE PANAMA CANAL

INTRODUCTION.

THE communication of the two great oceans by means of a canal is in no way a new idea. To-day it is considered to be the greatest of all modern undertakings, but the roots of the project lie far back in the history of the world. It is common knowledge that Columbus, by that rare intuition of genius that led him to discover the New World, always persisted in the idea of shortening the route to the seas of Asia in quest of the fabulous commerce in spices; this was the reason why, incited by the news that Vasco de Gama had found a passage south of the Cape of Good Hope, he set out in his fourth and last voyage with the sole purpose of discovering the route which he thought must exist. It so happened that he directed his course to the spot where such communication might possibly be found; in fact, to a place very near that in which the excavation of a canal is now in progress. But we shall pass over in silence the long and interesting history of the attempts made by Spain during the three hundred years of her domination over Central America. Nothing need be said with regard to the explorations carried out in the course of four centuries which led to the discovery of several possible routes, or the causes that ultimately contributed to the adoption of the Panama route. Such inquiries would be irrelevant to our subject.[1]

It would, however, not be possible, on the other hand, to understand the position of the Panama Canal before the law of nations without following closely the policy adopted by the United States in this connection, from the time that the great North American Republic came to be interested in the problem of this maritime communication. It is well known that the result of this policy has ultimately culminated in the construction of the canal under the control of the United States. We must therefore trace step by step the progress of this course of action, noticing thereby the changes and the tendencies manifested by the Department of State, in order that we may be enabled to state to what extent the privileges of neutralisation would attach, both in theory and in fact, to the waterway that will separate North and South America.

Objection may be taken to the treatment of the subject in this manner. In fact, it is hardly possible to avoid the criticism that the question is being dealt with from the political standpoint, leaving to its legal aspect only a secondary position. But it must be remembered that there can hardly be any conception that is not in some manner connected with another. In dealing with any given problem whose solution is sought, account must be taken of all those notions

[1] Information on the history of the proposition to unite the Atlantic and the Pacific by water communication may be obtained in the somewhat curious and discursive report presented to the Colombian Congress, on the subject of an interoceanic canal, by J. M. Quijano Otero, 1st April 1875.

that seem to be germane or have a bearing to it, if a masterly grasp of the subject is to be obtained, so as to reach the ultimate truth. It cannot be denied that International Law—which lacks that "positiveness" spoken of by Austin—is intimately connected with the science of politics and therein with diplomatic history. This is the reason why non‑dogmatic writers on the law of nations cannot avoid stepping into the domain of international politics. The states‑man has to appeal at every moment to precedent. He must know, if his arguments when dealing with an international question are to be of any avail, the existence of the rule of law, as well as the cases in which such rule was applied. Even for international jurists, whose business is not the actual dealing with concrete legal cases, the history of the law would seem to be necessary. As the law of nations is based on the *consensus* of the civilised states, their duty is to ascertain the agreement arrived at by the members of the international community. If instead of doing this they resort to *a priori* reasoning, then they will find themselves on some metaphysical height, whence they can only derive ethical principles that cannot under any possibility be regarded as legal rules. The jurist, therefore, in attempting to expand the law from the scientific point of view, is compelled to call the aid of history in order to ascertain the causes that have brought a certain rule into existence, and thus properly apprehend its application.

It is to be borne in mind that the conclusions at which we shall be able to arrive as regards the neutralisation of the Panama Canal are naturally influenced by the political action of the states most

directly concerned with the enterprise. For this
reason their diplomatic history in this connection
during the course of something more than three-
quarters of a century must be considered. But the
problem which these pages attempt to solve is
primarily legal.

Although it is not our intention to put forth, and
much less to reconcile, the various statements that
have been made purporting to contain the famous
doctrine of Monroe, as applied to an interoceanic
communication, it would seem advisable to begin this
study with the assertion of President Monroe in his
message of December 2, 1823. In this way we shall
be able to sketch out the position that the United
States have occupied and actually hold in the subject of isthmian transit across Central America. By
inquiring into the policy which the United States
have followed in this matter, much light will be
thrown on the subject of the position of the Panama
Canal before International Law.

In connection with the exorbitant claims in North
America on the part of Russia, who wanted to
appropriate to herself the dominion of land and sea
near Alaska, the United States President asserted
that the "American continents, by the free and independent condition which they have assumed and
maintain, are henceforth not to be considered as
subjects for future colonisation by any European
powers"; and under the circumstances connected
with the proposal of the Holy Alliance to help Spain
to regain her lost possessions in the New World,
Monroe expressed himself as follows: "We owe it
to candour and to the amicable relations existing

between the United States and the European powers, to declare that we should consider any attempt on their part to extend their system to any portion of this hemisphere as dangerous to our peace and safety." He went on to explain that the United States had no intention of interfering with the colonies and dependencies of European powers that then existed; but with regard to those governments which had declared and maintained their independence, "they could not view any interposition for the purpose of oppressing them or controlling in any manner their destiny by any European power in any other light than as the manifestation of an unfriendly disposition toward the United States."

These statements constitute what was the Monroe Doctrine. It is hardly necessary to say that they do not now cover the whole field that is generally supposed to be governed by the famous dicta of the American President. We shall be able to note the aspects which the Doctrine has taken in connection with interoceanic communications. Its flexibility has now become proverbial, and hence there can hardly be any reason for surprise if we observe that from negative assertions it has become a positive dogma of American foreign policy. But the question of the Monroe Doctrine, as a concrete problem, must be left here; for our duty is only to make clear the position of the interoceanic canal from the point of view of International Law.

PART I.

THE UNITED STATES AND THE INTEROCEANIC CANAL.

CHAPTER I.

ORIGINAL ATTITUDE OF THE UNITED STATES TOWARDS
THE CANAL QUESTION.

Soon after the independence of Central America had
been assured, interest was taken by this republic in
the construction of an interoceanic canal. As early as
1823 Señor Don Manuel Antonio de la Cerda urged
the matter upon the Federal Congress; but possibly
owing to the exhausted condition of the country in its
endeavour to overthrow the former government, no
steps were taken in this direction until two years
later, when Señor Antonio José Cañas arrived in
Washington as Minister of this republic. He at
once addressed a note to Mr. Clay, then Secretary of
State, drawing the attention of the United States to
the importance of uniting the Atlantic and the Pacific
Oceans by a canal through the country which he
represented. He further assured the Secretary of
State that his government would be extremely
grateful if the United States were to co-operate in
such a work, and that "it would be highly satisfactory
to have it a participator not only of the merit of the
enterprise, but also of the great advantages which
that canal of communication must produce, by means
of a treaty, which may perpetually secure the posses-

sion of it to the two nations." [1] Mr. Clay was undoubtedly personally interested in the canal project, but he was unable to commit the administration to any specific course with regard to this proposition. Nothing was known at that time of the feasibility of the enterprise. He, however, after consulting with the President, informed the Central American Minister that great interest was taken by the United States in the enterprise, and that he would give instructions to the newly appointed *Chargé d'affaires* to Central America, Mr. Williams, so that the latter would investigate the facilities which Nicaragua offered, and remit all possible data to the Department of State. It does not seem that the desired information was ever sent to Washington. [2]

A few months before, the United States had been invited to send representatives to the famous Congress of Panama, of 1826, where the delegates of the young republics would discuss the questions of common interest for the American nations. This invitation was formally accepted after a long debate in the Senate, but the object of the United States mission would have been defeated, even if the delegates had not been sent too late, because of the conditions and restrictions imposed on their powers. In the instructions of the American representatives to that Congress an announcement of the policy of the United States in reference to the canal is made for the first time. "A canal for navigation between the Atlantic and the Pacific Oceans," Mr. Clay wrote, "will form a proper

---

[1] Cited by Keasbey, *The Nicaragua Canal and the Monroe Doctrine*, p. 142.

[2] Sullivan, *Report on Interoceanic Communication*, p. 19.

subject for consideration at the Congress. That vast
object, if it ever should be accomplished, will be
interesting in a greater or less degree to all parts of
the world, but especially to this continent will accrue
its greatest benefits. . . . If the work should ever be
executed so as to admit of the passage of sea vessels
from ocean to ocean, the benefit of it ought not to be
exclusively appropriated to any one nation, but should
be extended to all parts of the globe upon the payment of a just compensation or reasonable tolls."[1]
It is clear from this that Clay's policy was that the
canal should be subject to control by none. But we
must observe that he did not express an opinion as to
the measures that should be taken in order to secure
to all nations the usage of the canal and the safety of
passage in case of war. It is possible, as is pointed
out by M. Achille Viallate,[2] that at that time the
United States would have readily acquiesced in an
understanding of the countries interested, so that the
neutralisation of the canal would be assured if the
scheme assumed practical shape. The fact that they
were then relatively weak as compared with the great
European powers, and that the Monroe Doctrine had
not as yet undergone a profound transformation, would
have contributed to an easy settlement for the protection of the canal by the more important nations,
without any objection on the part of the United
States, provided they obtained equality of treatment.

A few years later we find a European power
launching a project of a canal across Central America.

[1] Mr. Clay to Messrs. Anderson and Sargent, May 8, 1826;
Wharton, *Digest of International Law of the United States*, vol. iii. p. 1.
[2] *Essais d'Histoire Diplomatique Américaine*, p. 63.

The King of Holland, on account of his possessions
in Guiana, had taken a keen interest in Spanish
American affairs. He therefore sent General
Werweer to be present at the Congress of Panama.
The General, while on the Isthmus, showed himself
greatly concerned with the canal project. He studied
the enterprise on the spot, and on his return to
Holland he succeeded in forming a company, with
the king as its head, for constructing a canal through
Nicaragua. A contract was concluded with this
republic, whereby the canal was to be opened on the
same terms to all nations at peace with Central
America ; but armed ships were not to pass without
express consent, and this was never to be given to a
flag at war with another nation. The government
was to use its influence to have the neutrality of the
canal, and that of the ocean to a certain extent around
its termini, recognised by all the maritime powers.[1]
This seems to have been in accordance with the
American view, if indeed the United States had a
settled policy on the question of the canal at that
period. Mr. Huberich[2] is of opinion that the terms of
this contract entirely accorded with the views of the
Department of State. We know, however, that there
was some mild representation on the subject by Mr.
Livingstone, President Jackson's Secretary of State.
Mr. Jeffrey, the United States Minister to the
Netherlands, was instructed to inform the proper
authorities that the United States must be entitled
to all the advantages accorded to other nations. He
was further told to direct his endeavours to obtain for
either the people or the government of the United

[1] Sullivan, *op. cit.* p. 20.   [2] Huberich, *The Trans-Isthmian Canal*, p. 4.

States the majority of the shares of the Holland Company. The Dutch scheme, however, failed. The revolution in Belgium broke out, and the subsequent separation of that state from Holland put an end to the canal project.

The action thus taken by the United States gave new hopes to Nicaragua. She thought that, since the North American Republic had made representations to Holland at the time of the Dutch agreement, it was because the United States had fully perceived the importance of the question. The Federal Congress of the Central American Confederation therefore took action by making a generous proposition to the United States : they were formally offered the prior right, before all other nations, in the construction of the canal. Thus it is that, in answer to this liberality on the part of Nicaragua, we obtain on March 3, 1835, a resolution of the Senate of the United States in which the original policy of Mr. Clay is reasserted. The resolution is as follows :—

" That the President of the United States be respectfully requested to consider the expediency of opening negotiations with the governments of other nations, and particularly with the governments of Central America and New Granada, for the purpose of effectually protecting, by suitable treaty stipulations with them, such individuals or companies as may undertake to open a communication between the Atlantic and Pacific Oceans by the construction of a ship canal across the Isthmus which connects North and South America ; and of further securing for ever, by such stipulations, the free and equal right of navigation of such canal to all nations, on the payment of such reasonable tolls as may be established, to compensate the capitalists who may engage in such undertaking and complete the work."

In conformity with this resolution, President

Jackson appointed Mr. Charles Biddle to make the proper investigations on the Isthmus and report on the subject. The President gave an account of this mission in his message of January 9, 1837. He submitted to Congress that there was no probability of taking up the construction of the canal at an early date, and therefore he considered it inexpedient to enter into negotiations with foreign governments upon the subject.[1]

In the following year the question was again discussed in Congress. The Mayor of New York, and some members of that city and of Philadelphia, addressed a petition to that body pointing out the national importance of the construction of a maritime canal, and praying the aid of the State for such enterprise. This memorial was submitted to the Committee of Roads and Canals of the House of Representatives. Mr. C. F. Mercer, in his report of March 2, 1839, said : "It is obvious that if the contemplated communication from sea to sea be practicable, the nation which has the right to appropriate its exclusive use to itself might lawfully control the richest commerce of the world, or prescribe to all other nations the terms upon which they be admitted to share its enjoyment. The policy is not less apparent which should prompt the United States to co-operate in this enterprise liberally and efficiently."[2] The House of Representatives then passed a resolution similar to the one which the Senate had issued three years before.

In spite of the suggestive tenor of the report of Mr. Mercer, the new President, van Buren, contented

[1] *Messages and Papers of the Presidents*, vol. iii. p. 272.
[2] Sullivan, *op. cit.* p. 20.

himself with sending another agent to Central
America, who did not deem it expedient to undertake
the work at the moment, on account of the unsettled
and revolutionary state of the country. We need not
be surprised at the apathy evidenced by the United
States at this time. Van Buren, who was of the
same political creed as Jackson, followed also his
canal policy, which was no other than that of Clay.
The United States did not desire anything more than
the use of the canal, if it was ever constructed, under
the same conditions as it would be granted to all
other nations. The government itself seems to have
been somewhat slow in advocating the opening of a
route. In fact, the policy of the Department of State
was, with the cautious limitation just pointed out, of
the *laissez-faire* type, both because there does not
appear to have been a pressing demand for such an
enterprise as a State concern (even though this may
be limited to instigating private undertaking), and
also because the relative strength of the United States
did not urge politicians to a broader foreign policy
which, potentially at least, might encumber the administration.

But the acquisition of vast territories on the
Pacific side as a result of the war with Mexico, the
discovery of rich gold mines in California, and finally
the absence of direct means of communication, gave
a new impetus to canal projects. President Polk
instructed the American agent in Mexico, Mr. Trist,
to offer double the indemnity in case Mexico should
agree to grant to the United States the exclusive
right of transit across the Isthmus of Tehuantepec.
Mexico refused to concede this privilege.

About the same time (1846), the American *Chargé
d'affaires* at Bogotá was concluding a treaty of peace,
amity, navigation, and commerce with New Granada.
In this convention there appears a clause whereby
this republic "guarantees to the government of the
United States, that the right of way or transit across
the Isthmus of Panama, upon any modes of communication that now exist, or that may be hereafter
constructed, shall be open and free to the government
and citizens of the United States ; . . . and the United
States guarantee, positively and efficaciously to New
Granada, by the present stipulation, the perfect
neutrality of the before-mentioned Isthmus, with the
view that the free transit from the one to the other
sea may not be interrupted or embarrassed in any
future time while this treaty exists ; and in consequence, the United States also guarantee, in the same
manner, the rights of sovereignty and property which
New Granada has and possesses over the said
territory."

This was the first treaty concluded by the United
States that contains direct reference to trans-isthmian
transit.   Apart from this fact, the treaty itself contains
a provision that marks an epoch in the diplomatic
history of that country.   The protection tendered by
the United States to another country actually ran
counter to that traditional policy that "the fathers"
had bequeathed to future statesmen, and which had
always been regarded as the foundation - stone of
American foreign relations.   The guarantees of
neutrality over the Isthmus of Panama and of the
sovereignty of New Granada over that piece of
territory would, potentially at least, lead the United

States into embroilments abroad. Polk well knew this, but he also perceived the importance of taking a bold move, with the attendant dangers, if he was to facilitate to the nation the means of communication with the newly acquired regions on the Pacific. The fact is that he never gave instructions to his *Chargé d'affaires* at Bogotá for the insertion of the clause of guarantees. In his message to the Senate submitting the treaty he says that "the *Chargé d'affaires* acted in this particular upon his own responsibility and without instructions."[1] But Polk nevertheless assumed the responsibility, and transmitted the treaty to the Senate, where it was finally ratified without a dissenting vote.

It has now become known that Mr. Bidlack, the United States *Chargé d'affaires* at Bogotá, consented to the insertion of the clause of guarantees after perceiving the enormous benefits that his government would obtain thereby. The moral and material advantages that would accrue to the United States were pointed out to him by Señor Mallarino, the New Granada Minister of Foreign Affairs, in a confidential memorandum. It was common at that time, and to a certain extent it was excusable, to fear British designs in Spanish America. To counteract any aggressive tendencies that Great Britain might have had on the Isthmus, Mallarino urged on the American *Chargé d'affaires* the adoption of his plan. His good faith, and, perhaps, his lack of foresight, prevented the Minister from perceiving the difficulties that such a guarantee would create, and further the

---

[1] *Messages of the Presidents*, vol. iv. p. 511.

preponderant influence that it was bound to exert in the destinies of his country.[1]

It is of paramount importance for our purpose that we should consider the extent of the neutrality that the United States guaranteed according to this treaty, as interpreted by President Polk. " In entering into the mutual guarantees proposed by the thirty-fifth article of this treaty," thus runs his message, "neither the government of New Granada nor that of the United States has any narrow or exclusive views. The ultimate object, as presented by the Senate of the United States in their resolution to which I have already referred,[2] is to secure to all nations the free and equal right of passage over the Isthmus. If the United States, as the chief of the American nations, should first become a party to this guarantee, it cannot be doubted—indeed it is confidently expected by the government of New Granada —that similar guarantees would be given by Great Britain and France. . . . That either of these governments would embrace the offer cannot be doubted, because there does not appear to be any other effectual means of securing to all nations the advantages of this important passage but the guarantee of great commercial powers that the Isthmus shall be neutral territory. The interests of the world at stake are so important that the security of this passage between the two oceans cannot be made to depend upon the

---

[1] The memorandum is given at length in García-Merou, *Historia de la diplomacia americana*, tomo segundo, pp. 7 et seq.

[2] The resolution of the Senate alluded to is the one that we have quoted on p. 13, *supra*. The fact is, as Polk himself tells us, that he is following no other than the original policy of his country in connection with the subject of a trans-isthmian canal.

wars and revolutions which may arise among different nations." [1]

We may pause here for a while to consider the march of events in connection with this subject from the time in which the United States first came to show any interest in trans-isthmian communication up to the moment when the treaty with New Granada was ratified. It is easy to see that Polk completed Clay's policy, for the latter, although fully conscious of the importance of a canal communication and of the benefits that would thereby accrue to his country, did not venture, as has already been pointed out, to sketch out the scheme whereby the security of the route would be guaranteed to all nations. Special circumstances had been gradually influencing the course of events, and thus Polk could do nothing but adopt that line of action, unless he was to let the opportunity slip from his hands, proving thereby a patent lack of statesmanship. He had further the incitement of both the Senate and the House of Representatives, when, a few years before, the President had been requested to enter into negotiations with foreign governments for the effective protection of an isthmian canal. He adhered steadfastly to the view that the passage should be free to all nations, and that the equal enjoyment of it should be guaranteed by all the great commercial powers by means of a stipulation of neutrality. The United States did not, and indeed could not, aspire to the control of the route.

It would be hardly necessary to suggest that there is sufficient justification for the assertion that the

[1] *Messages of the Presidents*, vol. iv. p. 512.

United States were perfectly sincere in expressing this view at the time with which we are now dealing. Although the ambition for territorial expansion had already begun, they were not yet bold enough to demand the sole and entire control of such an important passage. On the other hand, no decisive steps had been taken by European powers so as to incite competition. It is true that from time to time a kind of theoretical interest in canal projects across the American Isthmus had been shown on the part of some of these states, but no practical measures had as yet been taken that would give foundation to the belief of a successful enterprise. As evidence of the sincerity of the United States that the passage should be free to all, it may be stated here that in a dispatch of December 14, 1849, to Mr. Lawrence, the American Minister at London, the Department of State requests him to co-operate with the Minister of New Granada in obtaining from the British Government a guarantee of the neutrality of the Isthmus of Panama, similar to that contained in the treaty concluded by the United States with that republic.[1] Such a step on the part of the United States would conclusively show that in fact they had not sought any exclusive advantages in signing the treaty referred to, in the event of the canal being opened across that part of the territory; for it is clear that if one of the European powers accepted the burden of guaranteeing the neutrality, it would

---

[1] Mr. Clayton to Mr. Lawrence; Sullivan and Cromwell, *Compilation of Executive Documents and Diplomatic Correspondence relative to a Trans-Isthmian Canal*, vol. i. p. 529. This work will be hereafter referred to as *Compilation of Documents*.

also claim the corresponding advantages secured by the United States in their treaty with New Granada.

Before noticing in this connection the subsequent events that radically altered the attitude of the United States towards the canal question, one should observe how the Department of State has interpreted the clause relative to the neutrality of the Isthmus, as contained in the treaty of 1846. Herein we shall incidentally notice another relaxation of the Monroe Doctrine. The United States have, it is true, gradually and effectively developed the policy advanced by their ablest and earliest statesmen, but in the course of this progressive evolution they have receded, on more than one occasion, from that original position. This result may, of course, be due to the changes of opinion that necessarily influence the conduct of the government, or to some unavoidable difficulties that the administration finds impossible to gauge in a manner different from that which, by means of a compromise, does away with the lofty idealism of the absolute principle. There is no reason for surprise, therefore, if we find these deviations from their traditional policy. Consistency has never been the golden rule of governments.

In the year 1862, in the course of one of those insurrectionary movements that unfortunately have been so common in what is now called Colombia, General Mosquera, the leader of the revolution, sent an armed force to occupy the Isthmus of Panama. Señor Herrán, Minister Plenipotentiary in Washington, invoked the aid of the United States in accordance with the provision of the treaty of 1846. In .con-

sequence, an American naval commander was instructed "to take care to protect and guarantee at all
hazards and at whatever cost, the safety of the railroad transit across the Isthmus of Panama." But as
Señor Herrán insisted that the security of the transit
could not be adequately ensured by the presence of a
mere naval force, and that New Granada was entitled
to the special aid of a land force to be sent by the
United States, the Department of State sought an
understanding with Great Britain and France as to
whether any proceedings taken by the United States
would meet with their assent and acquiescence. It
was further intended to discover whether these two
countries would co-operate with the United States in
a joint occupation of the Isthmus of Panama. It so
happened that the British and French Governments
did not see any ground for such an interference, and
thus the matter was dropped, and New Granada was
left alone to extricate herself from her own difficulties.[1] At this time the very integrity of the
United States was threatened, and Seward, just as
Clayton had done a few years before, in order to
save, as he thought, the administration, felt that the
best plan was to depart from the policy of his predecessors. This invitation from the United States
themselves to European powers in order to effect
a joint occupation in the New World was such a
patent disregard of the Monroe Doctrine, for which
all Latin America had had great reverence and
trust, that Mexico, whose independence was then
endangered by the coalition of Great Britain,
France, and Spain, protested against this uncalled-

[1] *Compilation of Documents*, vol. ii. pp. 1147 et seq.

for act as a violation of the dignity of Spanish America.[1]

Shortly afterwards the government of the United States was called upon to interfere, if the necessity should arise, to prevent the importation of troops and munitions of war by Spain across the Isthmus of Panama, for the purpose of carrying on a war with Peru. The necessity for such an interference did not arise; but the Attorney-General, to whom the case was referred for an opinion, held that under the guarantee promised by the United States in the treaty of 1846 such interference would be obligatory. Here we have a clear statement with regard to the interpretation of the neutrality of the Isthmus of Panama. The meaning attached by the Attorney-General to the term *neutral* in this connection was simply that the route should not be used by a state when its avowed purpose was to carry on a war.

After the recital of the above facts, it becomes unnecessary to dwell any longer on the question of the extent of the "neutralisation" bestowed on the Isthmus, as provided by the treaty of 1846. According to the views of the United States, this amounted to some kind of protection by means of which freedom of transit to non-belligerents would be ensured. At this comparatively early period of the history of neutralisation, the proper signification of the conception as applied to the thoroughfares of the world had not yet become clear, although there were, even then, sufficient manifestations to show that it

---

[1] *Diplomatic Correspondence*, 1863, p. 1150. See also *Annals of the American Academy of Political and Social Science*, July 1903, p. 119.

was in the course of formation. The laws of war were at that time in a very imperfect condition, and hence it was rightly feared that the mere approach of belligerents to a zone over which peaceful passage was to be maintained, was sufficient in itself to prevent the free transit. Add to this the strange misconception that inevitably resulted from the entirely different meaning of the term when applied to neutralised places over which no free passage is sought to be secured.[1]

It has been seen that up to the present the policy of the United States has been the construction of the canal by private enterprise and subject to political control by none. They have not sought advantages that would not be accorded in the same manner to other nations. It was partly because at this epoch they had not yet reached such a stage of development as would prompt them to launch projects that would arouse the susceptibilities of the Great Powers, and partly owing to the fact that there was hardly any need for the assertion of an advanced and agressive policy. In concluding the first treaty—which, as has been observed, was entered into without instructions from the Department of State—dealing with the transit between the two oceans, they were satisfied with the understanding that the passage would be for the common enjoyment of all nations.

[1] See *infra*, p. 105, note 1.

CHAPTER II.

THE CLAYTON-BULWER CONVENTION.

THE next important topic in connection with the history of the canal across the Isthmus is the conclusion of the Clayton-Bulwer Convention. It would not be possible, however, to understand its provisions without noticing first, at least succinctly, the events that led to its negotiation. The endeavours on the part of Great Britain to acquire possessions in Central America can be traced back to the end of the seventeenth century. A period of British encroachments then began, first on the Spanish colonies, and then on the Central American Republics, the successors of Spain. And by the year 1830 Great Britain may be said to have assumed practical control over the territory of Mosquitia.[1] Following the same line of action, the British Superintendent of Belize, a Mr. McDonald, in August of 1841, seized by force San Juan del Norte (Greytown) as part of the Mosquito territory. The action of McDonald and the outrages committed by him were not disavowed by the British ministry, in spite of the protests to Great Britain and the appeals to the world by the Central American States.

[1] Travis, *The History of the Clayton-Bulwer Treaty*, p. 31.

Even the United States paid these appeals no particular attention. Such proceedings, on the contrary, only incited Great Britain to take higher grounds than ever in defence of her pretensions. Thus on June 30, 1847, she formally laid claim to the contested territory, and early in 1848 had completely ousted Nicaragua.[1] By means of this aggressive stroke Great Britain was placed in a position to lay down the conditions under which the canal would be opened by the Nicaragua route, for one of its termini would necessarily be San Juan. It must be remembered that according to the generally accepted view of the time this was the most feasible communication for the desired waterway.

Great Britain's action could not but arouse a storm of indignation in the United States. Those who were more interested in the construction of the canal as a money-making enterprise saw in the British aggressions a commercial competition. They accordingly spread the news of the unwarranted encroachments, and endeavoured successfully to bring into prominence the Monroe Doctrine. The administration, on the other hand, had not only the pressure of the popular feeling, but perceived also in the British measure a clear and decisive opposition to the policy of the United States of a canal subject to control by none.[2] It is evident that, if the canal

[1] *The History of the Clayton-Bulwer Treaty*, pp. 37-42.

[2] Mr. Buchanan, who was then Secretary of State, sums up the situation thus : "The object of Great Britain in this seizure is evident from the policy which she has uniformly pursued throughout her history, of seizing upon every commercial point in the world whenever circumstances have placed it in her power ; and now it seemed her evident purpose, by assuming the title of protector over a miserable, degraded,

was to be controlled by a foreign power, the United States would have been practically at the mercy of that state which held the key to the passage. Under these circumstances the Department of State was left no alternative but to take prompt action.

Mr. Hise was therefore sent to Central America in order to investigate the validity of the British claims. His instructions, however, did not empower him to obtain any right in connection with the transit route. In spite of this he concluded, without authority, a treaty with Nicaragua whereby the exclusive right to construct the canal was conferred on the United States or their citizens. The United States were permitted to erect fortifications along the route and at the ports at either end; but, on the other hand, were bound to guarantee the integrity of Nicaragua.[1] This convention of course flatly denied the existence of the British claims.

It is important to remember in this connection that the Cabinet of Washington was not in a very satisfactory position. In fact, the nervousness of the Department of State was such that the diplomatic triumph of the United States Minister in Central America could only be regarded as an embarrassment. The Government did not, and in fact could not, desire the exclusive control of the waterway, or

and insignificant tribe of Indians, to acquire an absolute dominion over the vast extent of seacoast in Nicaragua, and to obtain control over the route for a railway and canal between the Atlantic and Pacific Oceans." Letter of instruction to Mr. Elijah Hise, Special Envoy of the United States to Central America, quoted by Keasbey, *op. cit.* p. 194.

[1] Hise-Selva Convention, June 21, 1849. Cp. J. G. Whiteley, "Les Traités Clayton-Bulwer et Hay-Pauncefote," *Revue de Droit International,* tome iii. seconde série.

burden itself with the further responsibility of guaranteeing the integrity of Nicaragua, to say nothing of the conflict with England that the approval of Hise's action would inevitably entail. The result was that the treaty was never ratified. The new administration of General Taylor, animated by a sincere desire of reconciliation, and anxious to avoid an international complication in which the United States would not have been on the winning side, recalled Hise, and his acts in this respect were summarily disavowed.

The ostensible views of General Taylor were unequivocally in favour of a canal free to all the world, under equal terms, and therefore subject to control by none. In his first message to Congress he says that the "territory through which the canal may be opened ought to be freed from the claims of any foreign power. No such power should occupy a position that would enable it hereafter to exercise so controlling an influence over the commerce of the world as to obstruct a highway which ought to be dedicated to the common uses of mankind." His administration, therefore, endeavoured to get the British Government to conclude a treaty with Nicaragua whereby both Great Britain and the United States would guarantee the safety of the transit, but no exclusive advantages would be conferred on either nation.[1] It is hardly necessary to suggest the reasons which prompted President Taylor to adopt this conciliatory tone. He was confident that in this way he could obtain from the British Government the adoption of a less aggressive

[1] Cited by Huberich, *op. cit.* p. 8.

policy with regard to Central American affairs. The idea firmly prevailed in the United States that Great Britain's intentions were no other than the acquisition of control over the projected canal.

It fell to the task of Mr. Lawrence, the United States Minister at London, to undertake the difficult negotiations. He, thinking that the continuance of the British occupation in Central America was dangerous to the peace of his country, insisted on the withdrawal of the British protectorate from the territory of Mosquitia, as a necessary condition for the settlement of the canal question. But Lord Palmerston, who was quite aware of the nervousness that his decision would cause in the United States, and wishing by all means to uphold the British claim, refused to accept the American proposal, and therefore nothing was done at London.

In the meantime the bitterness of feeling of the people of the United States as against Great Britain was growing more and more accentuated. The seizure of Tigre Island—the Pacific terminus of one of the possible routes—by the British inflamed the public mind. Mr. Clayton, the Secretary of State, became somewhat nervous, and then pressed on Sir Henry Bulwer, British Minister at Washington, to acquiesce in settling the matter there instead of at London, even though he was aware that the latter had no instructions to that effect. Sir Henry grasped the situation at a glance, perceiving that it was easier to deal with Mr. Clayton than with Mr. Lawrence. He therefore, assuming all the responsibility, but at the same time perfectly conscious of the discretionary powers possessed by high officials under special circumstances, wisely accepted the suggestions of the Secretary of State, and proceeded, with no small amount of foresight and judgment, to conclude the so-called Clayton-Bulwer treaty, which was ratified on July 5, 1850.[1]

The provisions of the treaty may thus be summarised :—

(i) Neither Great Britain nor the United States "will ever obtain or maintain for itself any exclusive control" over the canal.

(ii) Neither will they erect fortifications commanding the canal, nor occupy, colonise, or exercise any dominion over any part of Central America.

(iii) In case of war between the contracting parties the public vessels of either must be allowed to pass unmolested.

(iv) Great Britain and the United States promise to guard the safety and neutrality of the canal, and to invite all nations to do the same.

(v) The two governments "having not only desired, in entering into this convention, to accomplish a particular object, but also to establish a general principle, they hereby agree to extend their protection, by treaty stipulation, to any other practicable communications, whether by canal or railway across the Isthmus . . . and especially the interoceanic communications . . . which are now proposed to be established by the way of Tehuantepec or Panama."

It has been explained that the intention of the United States at that time was to prevent the intrusion of Great Britain in American affairs. Mr. Clayton was short-sighted in this respect, for, instead of having attained the end which he had in view, the real effect of the treaty was to legalise, at least in the opinion of some, the *status quo*, in so far as it related to British possessions in Central

[1] Letters of Sir Henry Bulwer to Lord Palmerston, *Compilation of Documents*, vol. i. pp. 555 et seq.

America that then existed. It was feared that if
the point at issue was not settled by means of an
agreement between the two powers, the Monroe
Doctrine would suffer a serious blow at the hands
of the British Government. But the administration,
considering itself to be placed in a dilemma, adopted
a line of action that actually ran counter to the
principle which it was sought to maintain. For
every word of this treaty, so to speak, constituted
a violation of both the spirit and the letter of that
policy which had been consecrated by all North
American statesmen. It seems therefore evident
that the feeble administration of General Taylor
thought that this was the only way of solving the
difficulty created by the aggressive conduct of Great
Britain in attempting to acquire the command of the
then proposed canal.

Two important facts must be noticed here, both
of which have a direct bearing on the question that
is being dealt with : (1) The neutrality of the canal,
by whatever route, was guaranteed by Great Britain
and the United States, both powers agreeing at the
same time to invite all other nations to guarantee
such neutrality. We say that the neutrality spoken
of by this treaty extended to whatever route should
be chosen for a canal which would be constructed
between the Atlantic and the Pacific Oceans, because
in the treaty itself the two governments made it
perfectly clear that their purpose was not only to
accomplish a particular object, but also to provide
for a general principle, thereby extending their protection, by means of treaty stipulations, to any other
route that might be chosen for the interoceanic

communication. The "protection" spoken of could not, of course, mean anything else than the guarantee of neutrality.[1] (2) The United States (and Great Britain also) stipulated never to obtain or maintain any exclusive control over the said canal. This provision proved to be a most potent estoppel to the policy which the United States were bent on pursuing, as we shall see, a few years later.

That the Clayton-Bulwer treaty did not satisfy the views of the United States is evident from the fact that very soon after its ratification controversies arose as to its proper interpretation. It is not necessary for our present purposes, however, to enter into a discussion of the disputes that arose on this point, or of the endeavours of both chancelleries to settle the differences. These seemed at one time so great that President Buchanan, unwilling to accept the suggestion of Great Britain that there should be a settlement by means of arbitration, was driven to state in his message to the Senate that "the wisest course would be to abrogate it" (the treaty) "by mutual consent, and to restore the *status quo ante*." Suffice it to say that the British Government sent in 1857 a special commissioner to Central

---

[1] It is interesting to note that the notion of neutralisation as applied to water communications had, by the time of the conclusion of the Clayton-Bulwer treaty, made a great advance, at least in the opinion of the statesmen who negotiated it. For it was expressly laid down that in case of war between the contracting parties the public vessels of either nation were to be allowed to cross the canal unmolested. It becomes evident, therefore, that if the provision whereby other countries would be invited to guarantee the neutrality of the route came into operation, then they would also be endowed with the same rights and burdened with the same obligations accorded by the convention. In fact, the neutrality of the route, had it then been opened, would have been perfectly binding.

America in order to negotiate with the different republics, and thus do away with the controversies arising out of the convention. Treaties were soon concluded with these states, so that by 1860 the difficulties seemed at an end.

While the controversies created by the Clayton-Bulwer treaty were being discussed, not without bitterness on both sides, there occurred an opportunity for the United States to attempt the acquisition of a kind of control over the passage by Panama, in the event of the canal being opened by that route. On account of the damage suffered by certain citizens of the United States in the course of the so-called Panama Riots of 1856, it was intended to secure from New Granada an indemnity by means of a convention. In the draft presented by the American Minister at Bogotá, it was proposed to include a provision in the treaty whereby both parties would be entitled to the right of passage across the Isthmus by any route that might be opened; and the said waterway was to be for the common use of all nations which would agree to regard the passage as neutral. It is to be noticed, however, that the United States were to acquire control over the route; for this purpose they intended to buy the islands in the Pacific which were near the terminus of the canal. Mr. Marcy, in giving instructions to the United States Minister at Bogotá, explained that in the event of his government obtaining "control of the road it would at once take measures to satisfy foreign powers that it would be kept for their common use on fair terms, and they would be asked to become parties with the United States

3

for a guarautee of the neutrality of that part of the Isthmus." [1]

It is evident that this proposal traversed the stipulations contained in the Clayton-Bulwer treaty. It was not necessary, however, that Great Britain should protest, for New Granada soon perceived the extent of the proposal, and, as it amounted to an injury to her sovereignty, flatly declined to give it any serious consideration.

It is thus seen what the policy of the United States had been up to the time of the Civil War. In preventing a European power from holding the key to the transit they had been on the verge of war, and were finally driven to conclude a treaty in which the Monroe Doctrine was consciously disregarded in every line. A few exceptions to the rule of a canal free from any political control are to be found during this period, but they are insignificant and can be easily explained away. The treaty which the enthusiastic Hise concluded with Nicaragua in 1849 had been entered into without instructions from the Department of State, and his acts were finally disavowed. With regard to the proposal of Mr. Marcy, although the ostensible purpose was the protection of the railway from Colon to Panama which had just been opened, and which, unfortunately, immediately suffered some damage by reason of the so-called Panama Riots, it is difficult to think that his object was not much wider. But, at any rate, it proved abortive.

[1] *Compilation of Documents*, vol. ii. pp. 1012 et seq

CHAPTER III.

A MORE important phase of the problem is now reached. The United States no longer follow their original policy of a canal for the benefit of all the world, under equal terms and subject to no political control of any kind. The condition which they have advocated, in order that there should be freedom of transit and safety both for the works of the canal and the persons using it, is that the passage should be regarded as neutral. But in the period with which we are now going to deal the United States have striven hard to obtain a kind of supremacy, a sort of political control over the waterway—in other words, their desires have been to obtain the key to the passage, so that they might be able to allow or refuse passage according as they thought that such permission or refusal would affect their political interests for good or for evil. In their exertions to follow out this course of action they have been hindered by the fetters which the previous policy had imposed upon them There have consequently followed supreme efforts to tear asunder these bonds. Their diplomacy in this direction has been as remarkable as it has been active. And although the arguments used have been more than once fallacious, yet the Department of State has issued documents of great plausibility and sometimes displaying extraordinary skill.

The new line of action came about as part of the broad and aggressive policy of Mr. Seward. The territorial expansion of the United States had already begun. They had won their victory over Mexico, and had exacted from her an important part of her territory. The internal affairs of the country, more-over, had been placed on a sure footing by the consolidation of the Union after the successful ter-mination of the Civil War. The Monroe Doctrine had just acquired great importance by warding off French interference in Mexico. In a word, the administration felt strong at home and respected abroad. If anything was at all necessary to awake a sense of self-importance in the United States, these circumstances proved to be more than enough. To them may be ascribed the birth of this more active and aggressive foreign policy. The United States, as we shall see, claimed to have absolute control over the canal across the Isthmus. It is hardly necessary to point out that the terms of the Clayton-Bulwer treaty were directly opposed to this policy. We shall have, therefore, to notice the endeavours of the Department of State to overcome the difficulties created by the reservations of this " entangling alliance."

The first move in this direction was taken by Mr. Seward himself. The project of a canal by Honduras had been revived. Mr. Seward hastened to conclude a treaty with this republic, and he contemplated the cession to the United States of Tigre Island to serve as a coaling station.[1] As this amounted, however, to acquiring control of the Pacific terminus of the canal, he directed Mr. Adams, his Minister at London, to sound Lord Clarendon as to the disposition of the British Government to favour the United States in acquiring coaling stations in Central America, notwithstanding the stipulations contained in the Clayton-Bulwer treaty.[2] In spite of the vague manner in which Lord Clarendon gave answer to this overture,[3] Mr. Seward saw that he must take a different course, and thus the Dickinson-Ayon treaty (1868) was concluded, in which the old view of a canal free to all and controlled by none is reflected.

But of course this was not what the United States were seeking at the time; they had to be contented with this meagre result on account of the liberal promises that they had been compelled, so to speak, to make to Great Britain in 1850. With extraordinary foresight, therefore, Mr. Seward looked farther down in the Isthmus and thought that he might obtain the desired advantages from Colombia, without directly wounding Great Britain's susceptibilities in Central America. In 1868 he began negotiations with that republic for a canal across the Isthmus of Panama, with the result that a treaty was signed at Bogotá on January 14, 1869. According to it the United States were empowered to construct the canal, having the peaceful enjoyment and control thereof. Colombia agreed not to allow the opening

---

[1] Keasbey, *loc. cit.* pp. 302 et seq.
[2] *Compilation of Documents*, p. 1183.
[3] *Ibid.* p. 1196.

of any other interoceanic canal or of any new railway through or across her territory from the Atlantic to the Pacific Oceans, without the express consent of the United States being first obtained. A stipulation with regard to the neutrality of the route is contained in this treaty: " The entrance to the canal shall be rigorously closed to the troops of another or others, including their vessels and munitions of war." This treaty was summarily rejected by the Colombian Congress.

On the appointment of Mr. Grant as President of the United States, Mr. Stephen A. Hurlbut was sent to Colombia in order to conclude a new treaty for the construction of the canal as a government enterprise. The result was the Treaty of Bogotá of January 26, 1870, by which the canal was to be opened to all nations at peace with both parties, on terms of absolute equality, but to be rigorously closed against the flags of all nations at war with either. The United States agreed to aid in protecting the canal against foreign attack and invasion. Mr. Hurlbut seems to have been extremely sanguine in his expectations that the treaty would be readily ratified by the Colombian Congress. Soon, however, he perceived that the matter was not so easy. The Colombian administration objected to a provision of the treaty whereby Colombia would make herself party in any war in which the United States should become involved. Señor Tapata, the Secretary of Foreign Relations, notified to Mr. Hurlbut that his government would insist on a radical change of such stipulation in view of the political complications that might result if the provision were to stand.[1] As it was expected, important modifications were introduced by the Colombian Congress. They so far traversed the views of the United States that the treaty did not prove acceptable to the Senate of this republic.

The diplomatic action of the Department of State became energetic soon after the grant made by Colombia to a private French company for the construction of the Panama Canal in 1878. The United States, no doubt, were jealous of this enterprise from the economic point of view. Endeavours, therefore, were made to undermine the French company by means of rival routes in Central America and Tehuantepec.[2] But the question really became of the greatest importance in its connection with the Monroe Doctrine. Under the later interpretations of this most flexible of all maxims, Monroe's dictum had gone beyond its negative assertions and adopted also positive principles as the guide of American diplomacy, whenever there was an opportunity for enhancing the moral supremacy of the United States. It was rumoured at the time that M. de Lesseps was inviting, on behalf of the French company, a coalition of European powers to guarantee and defend the

[1] In view of this fact there cannot be any reason for Mr. Hurlbut's strange supposition that the change of policy on the part of the Colombian Government was due to some petty ceremonies gone through by Mr. Bunch, Her Britannic Majesty's *Chargé d'affaires*. According to Mr. Hurlbut, "the change of policy was due, without doubt, to the action of Mr. Bunch. He had been exceedingly active for two weeks past, and used some rather strange means to deepen the hold he has on this people. For example, on Good Friday the British flag was displayed at half-mast, and Mr. Bunch attended every Mass at the cathedral, carrying a lighted candle in some procession which made part of the service" (*Compilation of Documents*, 1282).

[2] Keasbey, *op. cit.* pp. 362 et seq.

neutrality of the Isthmus. This necessarily, in the opinion of the United States, affected their traditional position in the New World. President Hayes hastened to impart his views to the world on the canal question and the Monroe Doctrine, in his message of March 8, 1880. The message is couched in unequivocal terms : " The policy of this country is a canal under American control. The United States cannot consent to the surrender of this control to any European powers." He urged that the canal would be the great ocean thoroughfare between the shores of the Union on the Atlantic and the Pacific, and "*virtually a part of the coast-line of the United States.*" [1] He concluded that it was " the right and the duty of the United States to assert and maintain such supervision and authority over any interoceanic canal across the Isthmus that connects North and South America as will protect our national interests." [2]

Views similar to those just quoted were also expressed by Mr. Evarts, Secretary of State, in his report presented to the President on the same date (March 8, 1880). This report was in answer to a petition of Congress, which seems to have been anxious for information on the French project. Mr. Evarts thought that the question was for his government " a territorial one, in the administration of which, as such, it must exercise a potential control." [3]

Mr. Evarts' energies did not stop here. In order to defeat the French project in its entirety, and to gain at the same time untold advantages for his

---

[1] The italics are our own.
[2] *Messages of the Presidents*, vol. vii. pp. 585, 586.
[3] *Compilation of Documents*, vol. iii. p. 1496.

country, thus carrying the Monroe Doctrine to the
extent which he thought it should have, he sought
to conclude a treaty with Colombia whereby it was
intended to declare that any concession for the execution of an interoceanic canal, heretofore made or
hereafter to be made by Colombia, was and should
be subject to the rights of the United States of
America as guarantor of the neutrality of the Isthmus
and of the sovereignty of Colombia over isthmian
territory, and that the consent of the United States
must be considered as a preliminary necessary to the
validity of any future grant or the modification of an
existing one.   It is hardly necessary to say that this
clause was designed for the purpose of doing away
with the contract between Colombia and the French
company.   The government of the United States
had already indicated its dissatisfaction with the grant
made without previously obtaining its consent, and
had also informed Colombia that, in the view of the
United States, the necessity for such consent was
and would be maintained as a consequence of the
guarantee undertaken by the treaty of 1846.   The
diplomatic tactics of Mr. Evarts were not sufficiently
veiled, and the result was that the Colombian Government disdainfully refused to consider a proposal for a
treaty whereby her right to grant such concessions
was questioned.[1]

In the meantime the question had been taken up
by Congress.   The views of the administration were
shared both by the Senate and the House of Representatives.   In the discussions that took place they
emphasised the opinion that was already current in

[1] *Compilation of Documents*, vol. iii. pp. 1513, 1534 et seq.

the political sections of the country, by recording in a resolution "that it is the interest and right of the United States to have the possession, direction, control, and government of any canal, railroad, or any other artificial communication to be constructed across the Isthmus . . . and in view of the magnitude of this interest, it is the duty of the United States to insist that if built, and by whomsoever the same may be commenced, prosecuted, or completed, and whatever the nationality of the corporators or the source of their capital, that the interest of the United States, and their right to possess and control the said canal or other artificial communication, will be asserted and maintained whenever in their opinion it shall become necessary."[1]

But it was clear to Congress that the greatest difficulty in the way of putting into practice the then national policy of the country was the Clayton-Bulwer treaty, that stood threatening, always ready to reduce to atoms any advances that tended to the acquisition of an exclusive control of the canal route—in fact, a powerful estoppel to the development of the Monroe Doctrine, in its new form, in connection with maritime communications across the Isthmus. Accordingly the Senate and the House of Representatives, on April 16, 1880, in a joint resolution requested the President to take immediate steps for the abrogation of the Clayton-Bulwer treaty.

President Garfield then came to power, and it fell to the lot of Mr. Blaine, his Secretary of State, to open the controversy. He showed himself greatly concerned on account of the rumours that were then

[1] *Compilation of Documents*, vol. iii. p. 1571.

current, that Colombia was seeking from the European powers some sort of joint declaration of the neutrality of the Isthmus of Panama. In order to protest against the contemplated action, if the reports were true, Mr. Blaine sent a circular dispatch to the United States Ministers in Europe. He dwelt upon the fact that his government had already in 1846 guaranteed the neutrality of the Isthmus, and that this guarantee did "not require re-enforcement, or accession, or assent from any other power." He said that the United States did not intend to interfere with the canal viewed as a commercial enterprise, or with the uses to which it might be put in time of peace. "It is as regards the political control of such a canal," continued Mr. Blaine, "as distinguished from its merely administrative or commercial regulation, that the President feels called upon to speak with directness and emphasis. During any war to which the United States . . . might be a party, the passage of armed vessels of a hostile nation through the canal at Panama would be no more admissible than would the passage of the armed forces of a hostile nation over the railway lines joining the Atlantic and the Pacific shores of the United States. . . . And the United States will insist upon her right to take all needful precautions against the Isthmus transit being in any event used offensively against her interest upon the land or upon the sea." The Secretary then declared that "an agreement between the European States to jointly guarantee the neutrality, and, in effect, control the political character of a highway of commerce, remote from them and near to us, *forming substantially a part of our coast-*

line,[1] and promising to become the chief means of transportation between our Atlantic and Pacific States, would be viewed by this government with the gravest concern." And again he uses more expressive language: "Any attempt to supersede that guarantee by an agreement between European powers, which maintain vast armies and patrol the sea with immense fleets, and whose interest in the canal and its operation can never be so vital and supreme as ours, would partake of the nature of an alliance against the United States." He concludes by warning his representatives at the European courts. "You will be careful in any conversation you may have," he tells them, "not to represent the position of the United States as the development of a new policy or the inauguration of any advanced, aggressive steps to be taken by this government. It is nothing more than the pronounced adherence of the United States to principles long since enunciated by the highest authority of the government."[2]

Mr. Blaine naturally insists upon the old argument of his country; it is true that the Monroe Doctrine is not mentioned (the Department of State in its diplomatic dispatches never speaks directly of the famous doctrine), but his reasoning is all based on it. It seems that he is tormented by the idea that his government has ever followed a liberal policy in connection with the canal question. We have seen what this policy was before the time of the Civil War.

---

[1] The italics are the author's.

[2] Mr. Blaine to Mr. Lowell, *Compilation of Documents*, pp. 1597-1602. This dispatch was sent *mutatis mutandis* to the other United States Ministers in Europe.

Mr. Blaine well knew this, and yet he boldly asserts that his line of action is not the development of a new policy. He also tells the United States Ministers, in a vein of plausible forgetfulness, or perhaps of inconsistency, that the guarantee of the neutrality of the Isthmus of Panama by the United States "does not require re-enforcement, or accession, or assent from any other power." He did not seem to have deemed it necessary to remember that Polk, speaking of this guarantee, had said that " it cannot be doubted . . . that similar guarantees will be given to that republic " (Colombia) " by Great Britain and France. . . . That either of these governments would embrace the offer cannot be doubted, because there does not appear to be any other effectual means of securing to all nations the advantages of this important passage but the guarantee of all commercial powers that the Isthmus shall be neutral territory." [1] Nor did the Department of State recall the fact that they had sent an invitation to the British Foreign Office to guarantee the neutrality of that part of Colombia. [2] Mr. Cass had also expressed the views of the Department of State in this connection when he told Lord Napier, British Ambassador at Washington, that " a similar measure on the part of England and France would give additional security to the transit, and would be regarded favourably, therefore, by the government of the United States." [3]

Even more worthy of note is the fact that Secretary Blaine seems to have ignored entirely

---

[1] See *supra*, p. 18.   [2] See *supra*, p. 20.

[3] Letter of Mr. Cass to Lord Napier, September 10, 1857, *Senate Ex. Doc.*, No. 112, 46th Congress, 2nd Session.

the existence of the Clayton-Bulwer treaty, for his dispatch was also sent to the British Foreign Office, Thus it is that Lord Granville in his answer confines himself to saying : "I should wish to point out to you that the position of Great Britain and the United States with reference to the canal . . . is determined by the engagements entered into by them, respectively, in the convention . . . commonly known as the Clayton - Bulwer treaty, and Her Britannic Majesty's Government rely with confidence upon the observance of all the engagements of that treaty."[1]

After expressing the views of his government with regard to the canal question in the general manner that we have seen, Mr. Blaine proceeded, before Lord Granville's dispatch had reached him, to deal with the Clayton-Bulwer treaty specifically, in compliance with the joint resolution of Congress. In a long letter to Mr. Lowell, the United States Minister at London, he indulged freely in an *ex parte* statement of the case, suggesting that the treaty should not be binding. He argued that the convention had been made over thirty years ago, under exceptional and extraordinary circumstances which had entirely ceased to exist. The United States had gone through a remarkable development on the Pacific coast, while the interests of Great Britain were inconsiderable in comparison with those of the Union. The real intention of the convention was to place the two parties on a plane of equality with respect to the canal, but under the present conditions

[1] Letter by Lord Granville to Mr. Hoppin, November 10, 1881, *Compilation of Documents*, vol. iii. p. 1622.

the effect of the treaty was to give the control of the canal to Great Britain by reason of her superior naval strength. He further insists : "This government, with respect to European States, will not consent to perpetuate any treaty that impeaches our rightful and long-established claim to priority on the American continent." He considered the case of a guarantee of the neutrality of the canal by the Great Powers of Europe, and very readily concluded that "the first sound of the cannon in a general European war would, in all probability, annul the treaty of neutrality," and that therefore "a mere agreement of neutrality on paper between the Great Powers of Europe might prove ineffectual to preserve the canal in time of hostilities." Mr. Blaine further drew from this, in the flexible manner of the logic of certain diplomatists, that the United States was the only power that could enforce " the absolute neutralisation of the canal as respects European powers," by asserting at the same time "her right to control the Isthmus transit." [1]

These were the reasons adduced by the United States Secretary of State for proposing essential modifications in the treaty—that is to say, that the United States should be allowed to fortify the canal and assume its political control. It is not difficult to think of the objections by which his arguments might be impeached. It must be remembered, however, that he had scarcely any ground for the controversy, and that nevertheless he plunged into the struggle for the abrogation of the treaty. Perhaps this is the

[1] Mr. Blaine to Mr. Lowell, November 19, 1881. This dispatch is given in full in *Messages and Documents*, 1881–1882, pp. 554–559.

reason why this letter of his has been called "one of the most remarkable state papers ever penned."

Lord Granville gave in due time a response to this note. He began by rightly pointing out that "the principles on which the whole argument of the dispatch are founded are, as far as I am aware, novel in International Law." He asserted that the interests of Great Britain in the canal are equal to those of the United States; and with regard to the unexampled development of the United States on the Pacific coast, Lord Granville said that "Her Majesty's Government cannot look upon it in the light of an unexpected event, or suppose that it was not within the view of the statesmen who were parties on either side of the Clayton-Bulwer treaty," and that such a change of conditions could not be accepted as a contention for "vitiating the foundations of an agreement which cannot be supposed to have been concluded without careful thought and deliberation." [1]

The two governments entered then into a discussion of the "historical objections" to the treaty, and here it may be safely stated that Mr. Blaine's part was decidedly weak. Lord Granville's acumen scattered the arguments of the United States Secretary of State.[2] It would be unnecessary to continue following the diplomatic wrangle that went on for a considerable time between the Cabinets of London and Washington; for Mr. Frelinghuysen succeeded Mr. Blaine in his post, and it was necessary

[1] Note of Lord Granville to Mr. West, January 7, 1882, *Compilation of Documents*, vol. iii. pp. 1646–1651.

[2] See letters of Mr. Blaine to Mr. Lowell, November 29, 1881, and of Lord Granville to Mr. West, January 14, 1882, *Compilation of Documents*, vol. iii. pp. 1633–1665.

for him, in view of the policy that the administration was bent on pursuing, to take up the American case and answer Lord Granville's dispatches. He found occasion, of course, to refer to "the traditional policy of the United States." But the reasonings on both sides to the dispute really amounted to expressions of opinion, and, as they were diametrically opposed, the controversy drew them further apart. Finally, Her Majesty's Government pointed out that if the Monroe Doctrine had not precluded the President and the Senate from sanctioning the treaty, how was it then that they came at this late date to say that it was opposed to their traditional policy?

The fact is, as we have already stated, that the Clayton-Bulwer treaty was a potent estoppel to this new policy of the United States in connection with canal communications. It was, in fact, a barricade which must, while in force, prevent them from obtaining an exclusive control over the route. The Monroe Doctrine—in its new form of not only preventing European powers from obtaining control over the New World, but of giving that control to the United States—must rest in abeyance until the difficulty was removed. It was not easy for the United States to come to this conclusion, especially as in their own point of view this doctrine was simply the national utterance of the right of self-preservation. But in the matter of the Monroe Doctrine, as applied to the transit question, Great Britain had undoubtedly throughout brought the better argument, and found, at that time at least, no reason whatever to depart from her views.

President Arthur was greatly concerned at the

4

French influence at Panama, and hence he attempted
to counteract this by the construction of a second
canal by way of Nicaragua.   Accordingly his administration took the bold step of negotiating a treaty
whereby it was provided that the canal should be
built by the United States of America and owned by
them and the Republic of Nicaragua ; and the former
power agreed to protect the integrity of the territory
of the latter.[1]   But Cleveland withdrew the treaty
from the Senate and it was never ratified.   In his
message of December 8, 1885, the President says :
" Maintaining, as I do, the tenets of a line of
precedents from Washington's day which prescribe "
(? proscribe) " entangling alliances with foreign states,
I do not favour a policy of acquisition of new and
distant territory or the incorporation of remote
interests with our own. . . . Whatever highway may
be constructed across the barrier dividing the two
greatest maritime areas of the world must be for the
world's benefit, a trust for mankind, to be removed
from the chance of domination by a single power, nor
become a point of invitation for hostilities or a prize
for warlike ambition.   An engagement combining the
construction, ownership, and operation of such a work
by this government, with an offensive and defensive
alliance for its protection, with the foreign state whose
responsibilities and rights we should share, is, in my
judgment, inconsistent with such dedication to universal and neutral use."[2]   President Cleveland in this
neat and precise language reverted to the ancient

---

[1] The Frelinghuysen-Zavala treaty of December 1, 1884.

[2] Message of Cleveland, December 8, 1885, *Compilation of
Documents*, vol. iii. pp. 1761 et seq.

policy of his country of a canal free from any political control ; he did not claim any exclusive advantages for his country, and did not feel tempted, therefore, to find fault with the Clayton-Bulwer Convention. His policy showed the prudence obtained from the experience of his immediate predecessors, who, in their desire to develop the Monroe Doctrine as applied to the canal question, had provoked a diplomatic controversy with Great Britain to find themselves only hopelessly defeated.

Generally after a stormy period there comes calm. This was the case with the United States immediately after the era of activity that terminated with the presidency of Mr. Arthur. The subsequent administration showed hardly any interest in the construction of the canal, and with regard to the "entangling alliance" with Great Britain no attempts were made to abrogate it. On the contrary, they found opportunity to cite the convention, showing thereby that they regarded it as still binding.[1]

[1] Cp. Viallate, *op. cit.* p. 136.

CHAPTER IV.

THE state of tranquillity or comparative stagnation in the policy of the United States as regards the canal question that came after the administration of President Arthur could not possibly last for long. The gradual development of the desires of the North American Republic to exert a kind of moral supremacy over the other nations of the New World could not be relegated to oblivion. The construction of the canal in itself, without obtaining its political control, would place great economic advantages in the hands of the United States citizens. But now they would not even obtain this, for it was evident that the Panama Canal would not be constructed by the French company. By the year 1888 the finances of the company became seriously embarrassed. Capitalists in the United States saw in this fact an opening for a new undertaking, and gradually they once more brought the question under the consideration of the government.

Moreover, subsequent events, quite apart from the influence brought to bear on public opinion by the commercial classes, forced the question into the field of governmental activity, and the construction of an interoceanic communication no longer appears as a subject for private enterprise, but as a work that should be taken up by the State itself. In spite of the supreme endeavours of the French company, the works at Panama had to be discontinued on account of the want of capital. The experience resulting from this fact tended to show that the canal could never be constructed unless vast resources were to be put at the disposal of the persons engaged in the operation. It was necessary, therefore, that a rich state should be ready to undertake the work. And there was nothing more natural than that the United States should consider themselves the most adequate nation for the completion of the enterprise.

About the time of the Panama Canal failure, an American company had been incorporated to start the construction of another canal by the Nicaragua route. This company, however, could not raise the capital necessary for the projected work. Early in 1891 a Bill was presented to Congress, under which the government was to guarantee an issue of bonds of this company to the amount of $100,000,000; and President Harrison went as far as saying :—

" I am quite willing to recommend government promotion in the prosecution of a work which, if no other means offered for securing its completion, is of such transcendent interest that the government should, in my opinion, secure it by direct appropriations from its treasury." [1]

On August 15, 1893, another Bill was introduced having the same object in view, but, like its predecessor, it never became law.

[1] President Harrison, annual message, December 9, 1891.

During his second Presidency (1893 tc 1897) Cleveland held the same liberal policy in connection with the canal as he had before, in spite of the change of opinion of the nation. And with regard to the Clayton-Bulwer treaty he could not but show satisfaction rather than displeasure. But at the Presidential Elections of 1896 the Republican party inserted in its programme a resolution to the effect that the canal should be "constructed, owned, and exploited by the United States." The candidate of this party was elected, but the new President, Mr. McKinley, made no mention of the subject in his inaugural address or in his first annual message (December 1897).[1]

But the war with Spain fully demonstrated to the people of the United States and to the administration the urgent need of a rapid communication between the Atlantic and the Pacific. At the commencement of the hostilities the *Oregon* had to make a long voyage round Cape Horn in order to come from San Francisco to the theatre of war. The annexation of Hawaii, and the enlargement of the possessions of the United States resulting from the war, brought even more importance to the question of maritime communications. Strategic, political, and economic reasons forced the problem, not so much as a convenience, but, to the mind of the United States statesmen, as a real necessity. Hence we find that Mr. McKinley expresses himself in his second message thus: "That the construction of such a maritime highway is now more than ever indispensable to that intimate and ready intercommunication

---

[1] Cp. Viallate, *op. cit.* p. 140.

between our eastern and western seaboards demanded
by the annexation of the Hawaiian Islands and the
prospective expansion of our influence and commerce
in the Pacific, and that our national policy now more
imperatively than ever calls for its control by this
government, are propositions which I doubt not the
Congress will duly appreciate and wisely act upon."[1]

It was only natural that this passage in the
message should excite much comment, and therefore Lord Pauncefote, the British Ambassador at
Washington, approached the Secretary of State on
the subject. He was assured that the United States
had no intention whatever to disregard the Clayton-
Bulwer Convention, but that in view of the strong
feeling prevailing to the effect that the canal should
be constructed by the government, they had to direct
their endeavours to obtaining from Great Britain
such a modification of the treaty as would, without
affecting the "general principle" contained in it,
enable them to accomplish the work.

Lord Pauncefote was immediately asked to consider a scheme of arrangement.[2] At that time (1899)
a Joint High Commission was sitting to discuss
various outstanding questions between the two
countries. The Foreign Office, it seems, thought
that they might obtain some advantages in settling
the question of the Alaskan boundary, which was
one of the points then considered by the Joint High
Commission; and thus the proposal of the United
States with regard to the canal was accepted.

---

[1] *Messages of the Presidents*, vol. x. p. 180.
[2] Cp. Dispatch of Lord Lansdowne to Lord Pauncefote, February
22, 1901, *Parl. Papers*, 1901 (Cd. 438).

Nothing, however, was agreed to in the question of the Alaskan boundary, but the Secretary of State urged his original suggestion for a new Canal Convention, and Great Britain, in a conciliatory disposition, accepted the consideration of the American plan.[1]

A treaty was entered into between Great Britain and the United States on February 5, 1900, but it did not prove acceptable to the Senate, and therefore some amendments were introduced which Her Majesty's Government did not agree to. But finally, on November 18, 1901, the two contracting parties signed the convention commonly known as the Hay-Pauncefote treaty. As this treaty supersedes the Clayton-Bulwer, and expressly provides for the construction of the canal "under the auspices of the government of the United States," it may be concluded that henceforth the policy of a canal subject to the control of the United States found free play. It is true that by this treaty all that was demanded by the North American Republic is not granted, yet the fetters that compelled the administration to remain in a state of inaction were removed.[2]

As soon as the above convention was definitely signed, the administration proceeded to take steps for obtaining the necessary privileges from the country through which the canal was to pass. The Isthmian Canal Commission had already studied the

[1] Cp. Dispatch of Lord Lansdowne to Lord Pauncefote, February 22, 1901, *Parl. Papers*, 1901 (Cd. 438).

[2] What has been said of the Hay-Pauncefote treaty in this connection would be enough for our present purposes. We shall have occasion, however, to deal with its provisions in detail when we come to consider the question of the neutrality of the canal in a more specific manner. See *infra*, pp. 107 et seq.

advantages of the different routes, and on its final report Congress passed a law authorising the Executive to buy the property of the *Nouvelle Compagnie du Canal de Panama*, and to acquire from the Republic of Colombia, for a reasonable consideration, the right to construct and exploit the canal, together with the perpetual control over the route. In case the President could not acquire from Colombia the necessary powers, he was authorised to take measures for the construction of the canal by Nicaragua.

The government of the United States was fully convinced of the superiority of the Panama route over that of Nicaragua, and this was one of the reasons why the administration showed itself so anxious for the acquisition of the necessary powers for the construction of a maritime communication by Panama. To what extent the United States have gone in this direction we shall shortly see.

It fell to the task of Mr. Hay, the Secretary of State, to enter into negotiations with Colombia. The fact that this republic was then in the midst of internal disturbances, and, consequently, the government was in a more than feeble position, greatly contributed to bring up serious difficulties in the way of the negotiators. It has been suggested by some that the exactions of Colombia, relative to the pecuniary indemnity that she expected in exchange for the concessions that would be granted to the United States, seemed for a moment to have done away with all hope of agreement. But on January 22, 1903, Señor Herrán, for the Republic of Colombia, and Mr. Hay, for the United States of America, signed a treaty for the construction of the canal. The treaty granted to the United States the exclusive right to construct, exploit, and protect the waterway and the works connected with it. The territory within the zone of the canal was declared to be neutral by the two contracting parties, the United States being charged to guarantee its neutrality, as well as the sovereignty of Colombia over the said territory. Colombia further gave authority to the United States to assure the protection and security of the canal, to maintain order and discipline among the persons engaged in the work, and also for the application of sanitary arrangements and of police which they thought necessary to ensure order and public health. As a consideration for these concessions, Colombia would receive from the United States, on the ratification of the treaty, the sum of $10,000,000 and the further annual sum of $250,000, to begin after nine years of ratification.

The Hay-Herrán Convention was duly ratified by the Senate of the United States. But the fate of the treaty became somewhat dubious when it came to be discussed in Colombia. The government had invited the public to express through the press their opinions concerning the treaty. It was evident that the people at large would not give a very favourable verdict, for it must be remembered that Latin Americans are more than suspicious when a question of sovereignty is to be entrusted to a powerful neighbour whose expansive designs they deem clear. Doctor Marroquín, the Colombian President, well knew the immediate effect of the invitation which he tendered to the people. On the other hand, he had a favourable Congress, which—it is thought by some—would have ratified the treaty if he had really desired it. It is well known that the negotiations were started by Colombia—that is, by Doctor Marroquín's administration. These considerations would tend to suggest that the President did not know exactly what to do under the circumstances, and that in his endeavours to escape from the dilemma in which he was placed he adopted the dangerous policy of treating *ad referendum* with a government that was not ready to be patient in a matter that was regarded as of supreme importance.

The treaty was submitted to the Senate in due course. The question of the restriction of the Colombian sovereignty over the canal zone came immediately to the front of the discussion. According to the fundamental laws of Colombia, the national jurisdiction cannot be restricted without effecting a change in the Constitution; hence this was the ground taken by the Senate in its demand that certain amendments should be adopted tending to avoid, as far as possible, the restriction of the national jurisdiction that would result if the treaty was to be ratified as it originally stood.[1] It is only fair to add that it has been the expressed opinion of some that this was only a pretext of the Colombian Senate in order to protract the negotiations, with a view to obtain a more substantial compensation for the rights which they were granting. But it may be pointed out that even if the question of the indemnity had its influence in

---

[1] Cp. *Canal de Panamá. Documentos relacionados con este asunto que se publican por orden del Senado de la República.* Bogotá, Imprenta Nacional, 1903.

the action of the Senate, it would be unreasonable,
to say the least, to suggest that this was the principal
cause in the rejection of the treaty.   Whatever faults
or shortcomings Spanish Americans may have in
connection with public or civic duties, they are
extremely jealous of foreign encroachments on their
sovereign rights, and, therefore, they cannot but regard
with anxious care a measure that not only would
curtail the national jurisdiction, but supplant it as
the necessary result of the coexistence of two public
powers in a given territory, the one national, the
other foreign.

It is possible, perhaps probable, that the treaty in
question would have been ratified by the Colombian
Senate with amendments that would have been
acceptable to the United States, if it had not been
for the impatient and even violent diplomacy of Mr.
Beaupré, the American Minister at Bogotá.[1]   For
everybody in Colombia knew that the President of
the United States was empowered by Article 4 of
the Spooner Act[2] to take steps for the construction
of the canal by Nicaragua if he failed to obtain the
necessary concessions from Colombia.   This provision
of the Spooner Act was naturally regarded as a
sanction which would operate and thus deprive
Colombia of the advantages of having the canal
constructed across her territory.

In a note of April 24, 1903, the American
Representative notified the Colombian Minister of

---

[1] This view is clearly expressed by General Reyes, Special Minister
of Colombia to the United States, in his dispatch to Mr. Hay,
December 23, 1903, *For. Rel.*, 1903, 284.

[2] See *supra*, p. 57.

Foreign Affairs that "any modifications would be in violation of the Spooner Act, and therefore inadmissible." And although it is a recognised principle of the Law of Nations that no breach of faith is committed by the refusal of a state to ratify a treaty entered into by its duly accredited agent, since the validity of a conventional engagement depends on the ratification,—the period granted for the exchange of ratifications being regarded as necessary for further consideration during which there exists the so-called *locus pœnitentiæ*,—yet, in spite of this just and reasonable legal rule, the United States Minister, in his memorandum of June 13, 1903, tells the Colombian Minister of Foreign Affairs that "the government of Colombia to all appearances does not appreciate the gravity of the situation." And he assures him further, in threatening form and substance, "that if Colombia now rejects the treaty or unduly delays its ratification, the friendly relations between the two countries would be so seriously compromised that our Congress might next winter take steps that every friend of Colombia would regret with sorrow." And again on the 5th of August he proceeds to say (*inter alia*) that "if Colombia truly desires to maintain the friendly relations that at present exist between the two countries, and at the same time to secure for herself the extraordinary advantages that are to be produced for her . . . the present treaty will have to be ratified exactly in its present form without any amendment whatsoever."

When we take into consideration the attitude of the American Minister at Bogotá, as well as the prevailing rumour that if the canal treaty fell through, the Department of Panama would declare its independence from Colombia, or that, if this did not happen, the canal might be constructed by Nicaragua, we may well discard entirely the view that the main cause for the rejection of the treaty was due to the desire for a larger compensation. We must take into account for the solution of this complex and intricate question the excitement that " the pressure of threats so serious and irritating " was bound to produce on the national sentiment—such threats as those of the American Minister which were intended to seek the immediate ratification of the treaty, but, obviously enough, contributed, in our opinion, to its disapproval.

It would be well to consider the concealed policy of the United States in case the canal treaty should not be ratified by Colombia. It is natural that when an event is likely to happen human foresight should begin to consider what would be the situation created, as well as the various possibilities by which that situation might be improved. The government of the United States was in one of those positions about the month of August 1903, when it began to appear probable that the Colombian Senate would not ratify the treaty. Under the circumstances the American Government attempted to find the various courses of action open to the United States. The administration was convinced of the superiority of the route by Panama, and hence it was ready to put into play all its ingenuity in order to carry out its plan. If this endeavour should have been successful, there would have resulted what may be regarded as a patent disregard of the strict principles of equity or justice.

It was not considered difficult to find a *prima facie* plausible reason to justify a measure that would have been, in fact, nothing less than a flagrant violation of the recognised rights of a sovereign community. An unparalleled flexibility in the interpretation of the treaty with Colombia of 1846 [1] was thought to be sufficient to deprive this country of her territorial rights, and thus furnish one of the possible courses of action of the United States. President Roosevelt is quite clear in his special message of January 4, 1904. "It was the opinion of eminent international jurists," says the message, "that in view of the fact that the great design of our guarantee under the treaty of 1846 was to dedicate the Isthmus to the purposes of interoceanic transit, and above all to secure the construction of an interoceanic canal, Colombia could not, under existing conditions, refuse to enter into a proper arrangement with the United States to that end without violating the spirit and substantially repudiating the obligations of the treaty the full benefits of which she has enjoyed for over fifty years. My intention was to consult the Congress as to whether under such circumstances it would not be proper to announce that the canal was to be dug forthwith; that we would give the terms that we had offered and no others; and that if such terms were not agreed to we would enter into an agreement with Panama direct, or take whatever other steps were needful in order to begin the enterprise." [2]

[1] See *supra*, p. 16.

[2] Special message of President Roosevelt, January 4, 1904, Moore, *A Digest of International Law*, vol. iii. p. 61.

This is evidently an astounding proposition, and for this reason it can well be thought that it could have never been seriously entertained by American statesmen.[1] But the contrary view becomes apparent when we remember the violent and threatening remarks of the United States Minister at Bogotá (he necessarily would have authority to serve such formal notifications in case the Colombian Senate felt inclined to refuse its approval of the convention),[2] as well as the consideration that the announcement of this course of action came when it was not necessary for the United States to take such drastic measures. This latter fact alone would tend to show that the proposal had been fully considered, and that it was found perfectly justifiable in the eyes of the administration; for otherwise the President would not have felt prompted to make such utterances which were not then really called for, and which might excite historical criticism and display to the world nothing less than an advanced form of imperialistic policy, arousing thereby strong suspicion among the other republics of the American continent.

After the rejection of the Hay-Herrán treaty by the Colombian Senate, events succeeded one another with extraordinary rapidity.[3] The members of the Congress for Panama were in favour of a canal treaty. It became evident to the government of Colombia that there was imminent peril of the

[1] This is the opinion of M. Philippe Bunau-Varilla, " La Question de Panama," *Nouvelle Revue*, April 15, 1904.

[2] See *supra*, p. 61.

[3] Full information as regards the independence of Panama is to be found in Rougier, " République de Panama," *Revue Général de Droit International Public*, tome xi. pp. 567 et seq.

Isthmus of Panama declaring its independence. In fact, during the months of September and October there were persistent rumours of secession both at home and abroad. In a cablegram from San José, Costa Rica, of August 31, published in the *Washington Post*, it is asserted that the Isthmus would soon be in open revolt against Colombia for its failure to ratify the Canal Convention. In the meantime the same fear was felt at Bogotá, for Senator Perez y Soto made a proposal to ask the executive to appoint an anti-secessionist Governor of Panama. Several speakers in the Senate said that Señor de Obaldía, who had recently been appointed Governor of that region, and was favourable to the canal treaty, was a menace to the national integrity.

It was well known that there were representatives of strong interests in New York prompting the secession of the Isthmus.[1] Doctor Manuel Amador Guerrero was in that city considering a plan of action for bringing about a revolution and forming an independent government. It is impossible to say to what extent, if at all, representatives of interests in Panama made overtures to the Washington Cabinet in order to ascertain the specific course that the United States would take in the event of a revolution for the independence of the Isthmus. We can only be guided in our conclusions by the overt acts of the United States rather than by confidential declarations, because, if any were made at the time, none have been made public up to the present.

On October 20, Doctor Amador Guerrero left New York for Panama with the purpose of put-

[1] See *The New York Herald*, September 10, 1903.

5

ting into action a plan for the entire separation of the Isthmus from the government of Colombia. On November 3, the people of Panama declared themselves an independent state, without the firing of a single shot. It is extremely suggestive and worthy of note, as M. Viallate remarks, that on October 19, the day before Doctor Amador left for Panama, the Navy Department of the United States issued instructions to the effect of having vessels within easy reach of the Isthmus in the event of a revolt taking place there, and thus endangering the safety of the transit that the United States were bound to insure by virtue of the treaty of 1846. On October 30, the *Nashville* was ordered to proceed to Colon; and on November 2 — the day before the proclamation of the independence of the new Republic — the following instructions were sent to the *Boston*, the *Nashville*, and the *Dixie* :—

" Maintain free and uninterrupted transit. If interruption is threatened by armed force, occupy the line of railroad. Prevent landing of any armed force with hostile intent, either government or insurgent, at any point within fifty miles of Panama. Government forces reported approaching the Isthmus in vessels. Prevent their landing if, in your judgment, the landing would precipitate a conflict."

According to General Reyes, "a military officer of the Government of the United States stopped the railway from carrying to Panama, as it was under obligation to do, a battalion that had just arrived at Colon from Bogotá at the very time when its arrival in that

MAP OF THE PANAMA CANAL ZONE.

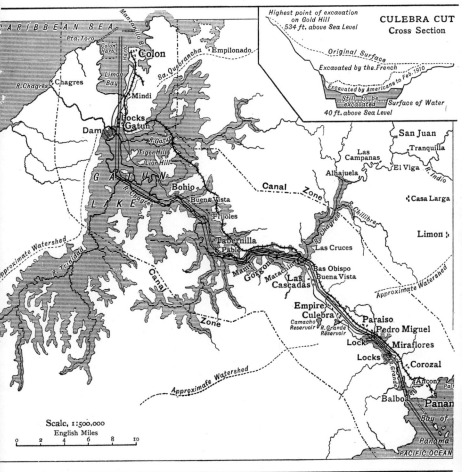

Emery Walke

city would have impeded or suppressed any revolutionary attempt." [1]

A few days after the declaration of independence, the United States recognised the *de facto* government, and on November 13 the President fully recognised the Republic of Panama, and formally received her Minister Plenipotentiary.[2]

On the 18th of the same month a treaty was signed by the two governments, whereby the United States obtained a monopoly for the construction of any system of communication by means of a canal or railroad, and bound themselves to guarantee the independence of the new state. The Republic of Panama grants to the United States in perpetuity " the use, occupation, and control of a zone of land and land under water for the construction, maintenance, operation, sanitation, and protection of the said canal." The Republic of Panama further grants to the United States "all the rights, power, and authority within the zone mentioned . . . which the United States would possess and exercise if it were the sovereign of the territory, . . . to the entire exclusion of the exercise by the Republic of Panama of any such sovereign rights, power or authority." There is a declaratory provision whereby it is said that the canal shall be neutral in perpetuity, upon the terms of, and in conformity with, the stipulations entered into by the United States and Great Britain in the Hay-Pauncefote treaty. The United States

---

[1] Note of General Reyes to Mr. Hay, December 23, 1903, *For. Rel.*, 1903, pp. 284 et seq.

[2] Mr. Hay, Secretary of State, to all U.S. dip. representatives, circular telegram, November 14, 1903, Moore, *op. cit.* vol. iii. p. 55.

shall have the right to use its police and its land and naval forces, or to establish fortifications in case it should become necessary for the safety or protection of the route.

This was the climax of a long series of attempts to put into practice the will of the American people. Many have been the endeavours and many have been the difficulties which they have encountered in their efforts to obtain the necessary powers for the construction of an interoceanic canal subject to the control of the United States.

CHAPTER V.

THE INTEROCEANIC CANAL AND THE MONROE DOCTRINE.[1]

THE different courses of action in the policy of the United States in relation to the interoceanic communication have now been traced to their sources. It may be interesting, at this stage of our inquiry, to attempt to summarise the general principles, and, if possible, to ascertain the tendencies underlying that policy. There can be no doubt that the question well deserves examination, for, even if such principles do not directly help us to draw purely legal conclusions with regard to the position of the canal, they certainly throw as much light on the interpretation of the international agreements that are supposed to govern the status of the waterway as all the other argumentative analogies that may be brought forward in this connection.

[1] Cp. Alvarez, "L'histoire diplomatique des Républiques américaines et la Conférence de Mexico," *R.D.I.P.*, t. ix. ; Antokoletz, *La doctrine de Monroë et l'Amérique latine* ; Delarüe de Beaumarchais, *La doctrine de Monroë* ; Latané, *Diplomatic Relations of the United States and Spanish America* ; Mérignhac, "La doctrine de Monroë à la fin du xixe siècle," *Revue du droit public*, 1896 ; Moye, "L'imperialisme américain et la doctrine de Monroë, *R.D.I.P.*, t. xii. ; Scott, "The United States and Latin America," *The Times* (South American Supplement), Nov. 29, 1910 ; leading article on the Monroe Doctrine in *The Times* (South American Supplement), Nov. 29, 1910.

At the outset it is of importance to note that the principles contained in the Monroe Doctrine are supposed to rest, according to the view of certain American authorities, on the right of self-preservation—a right that subordinates itself to no other, and whose sphere the domain of law can never attempt to curtail. Those who hold this opinion seem to have merely noticed the original intention of President Monroe of preventing the powers that formed the Holy Alliance from restoring to Spain her lost colonies in the New World. It was under these circumstances that he declared that any attempt on their part in this direction would be "dangerous to the peace and safety" of the United States.

It will be profitable to quote here the words of an American authority on the question of the Monroe Doctrine. Mr. Dana, in his edition of Wheaton's *Elements of International Law*, lays down the matter in this manner :—

"As a summary of this subject, it would seem that the following positions may be safely taken: I. The declarations upon which Mr. Monroe consulted Mr. Jefferson and his own cabinet related to the interposition of European powers in the affairs of American States. II. The kind of interposition declared against was that which may be made for the purpose of controlling their political affairs, or of extending to this hemisphere the system in operation upon the continent of Europe, by which the Great Powers exercise a control over the affairs of other European States. III. The declarations do not intimate any course of conduct to be pursued in case of such interpositions, but merely say that they would be 'considered as dangerous to our peace and safety,' and as the manifestation of 'an unfriendly disposition towards the United States,' which it would be impossible for us to 'behold with indifference'; thus leaving the nation to act at all times as its opinion of its policy or duty might require. IV. The declarations are only the opinion of the administration of 1823, and have acquired no legal force or sanction. V. The United States has never made an alliance with, or pledge to, any other American State on the subject covered by the declarations. VI. The declaration respecting non-colonisation was on a subject distinct from European intervention with American States, and related to the acquisition of sovereign title by any European power, by new and original occupation or colonisation thereafter. Whatever were the political motives for resisting such colonisation, the principle of public law upon which it was placed was that the continent must be considered as already within the occupation and jurisdiction of independent civilised nations."[1]

It will seem that the original idea was not entirely to exclude European influence from America, for, if this had been the case, it could never have been possible to secure the cordial assent of England to this principle. It must be remembered that it was Canning, England's Minister, who first attempted to put a check to the proposed policy of the allied powers. He saw that the endeavours of the Holy Alliance would amount to a death-blow to British traders, who were then advantageously speculating with the young republics.

England had been invited by the powers to join them in their measures in favour of Spain, but Canning, instead of giving a ready answer, imparted the matter to the Representative of the United States at the court of St. James, suggesting at the same time that the two governments should unite in defending the liberty of the Spanish American States by issuing a clear and forcible joint statement of their policy. There was a considerable delay in

[1] Wheaton, *Elements of International Law*, Dana's edition (Boston, 1866), p. 112.

the transmission of the proposal to the Department
of State, and therefore Canning, annoyed by failure
to secure the co-operation of the North American
Republic, decided to proceed alone. He at once
made known to Prince Polignac, France's Ambassador
at London, the determination of the British Government to oppose the interference of the Holy Alliance
in Spanish America.

It was only after England's declaration of policy
that the famous statement in the message of Monroe
was made public. It is only natural, therefore, to
suppose that the powers engaged in behalf of Spain
could perceive in the President's message the
British determination, and the sanction of the
Doctrine became, of course, more effective.[1]

But the other principle contained in the message,
relative to the prevention of future colonisation by
any European power, had never been discussed
between England and the United States. Its origin
is due, as has been observed, to the exorbitant claims
of Russia in order to appropriate to herself the vast
extent of land and sea near Alaska. This proposition
was not therefore favourably received in England.

It follows from this that Monroe's dicta, in fact,
had reference only to preventing the extension of
monarchical rule to the New World, and in declaring
that the American continents should not be considered
as subjects for future colonisation by any European
power. It was only natural, taking into account the
ideas and practices of the time, to suppose that the
extension of European dominions to America would

[1] See Wheaton, *Elements of International Law*, Dana's edition,
pp. 97 et seq.

imperil the peace and safety of the United States. From this point of view, therefore, it is correct to assert that the doctrine *was* a principle of self-preservation. But, under the present state of affairs, it would be to stretch unduly the ordinary signification of terms if the same statement were made to apply to the actual condition of things.

As emotions can only exist in the mind, they are difficult to fathom. The actions that may be taken in order to obtain self-preservation can only have their source in fear. To what extent this fear would be justified is not easy, indeed extremely difficult, to tell. But even then the line must be drawn somewhere. Nobody would attempt to suggest that there was not a potential danger for the security of the institutions of the United States when the Doctrine, as has been laid down, was enunciated. On the other hand, opinions must differ when it is intended to apply the same doctrine to the case of the treaty with New Granada of 1846. We have already pointed out that the clause whereby the United States promised to guarantee the neutrality of the Isthmus of Panama and the sovereignity of Colombia over that territory, was due to a potential fear that Great Britain might have designs on that part of America.[1] Now, if this clause had its origin in the possibility of British intervention there, why should the United States themselves seek that very interference of Great Britain and France a few years later? Why should they attempt to obtain that privilege instead of warding it off by a clear expression of policy?[2]

[1] See *supra*, p. 17.   [2] See *supra*, p. 22.

The Clayton-Bulwer treaty might be considered, from one point of view, to be a reassertion of the principles contained in the Monroe Doctrine, for its intent was to counteract the British progress in Central America. But in doing this, it must be remarked, the treaty actually legalised the British intervention, and also granted to the United States a special interest in the canal question. It seems as if the idea had been not only to ward off European interference, but also to give to the United States the privilege of interfering themselves.

The same suggestion is again possible in dealing with the abortive proposals of Mr. Marcy,[1] Mr. Seward,[2] and President Grant.[3] It was evident that the United States had already gone beyond, or at least extended the meaning of, self-preservation. They were under the fetters imposed by the Clayton-Bulwer treaty, by means of which the canal was to be free to all, and its neutrality guaranteed by the maritime powers. What danger could result from this to the "peace and safety" of the North American Republic? Could this guarantee in any way open the way for future colonisation or for implanting "European systems" of government in the New World?

It is likely that in the opinion of some there might be a possibility—they may perhaps say probability—for the gradual advance of European influence in American affairs if these powers were permitted, even in theory, to obtain advantages in the New World similar to those which the United States may enjoy. They may even find the same justification for the

[1] See *supra*, p. 33.   [2] See *supra*, pp. 36 and 37.   [3] See *supra*, p. 38.

later declaration of the United States of 1880, to the effect that their policy was a canal under American control, and that they could not consent to the surrender of this control to any European power. But even in the restricted sphere of the Monroe Doctrine which it is our duty to examine—that is, in its connection with the canal question—many more are the examples of intervention that have been accomplished under the cover of a Doctrine whose ostensible purpose is to ward off intervention.

Obvious instances of the above fact can be easily brought to mind. Mr. Evarts attempted to restrain Colombia from observing the fulfilment of the contract entered into by her with a French company for the construction of the Panama Canal, simply, it appears, because the work was not in American hands.[1] Mr. Blaine, as we have seen, followed a very aggressive policy. In order to protest against the projected action of Colombia that the canal should be neutralised by all maritime powers, he asserted his interpretation of the Monroe Doctrine. He thought that any such guarantee by the European powers would endanger the safety of the Union, for, in his opinion, during any war to which the United States might be a party, the passage of armed vessels of a hostile power through the canal would be no more admissible than the passage of hostile forces over the railway lines of the United States, and hence he concludes that they must insist upon taking "all needful precautions against the Isthmus transit being in any event used offensively against her interest."[2] Both Mr. Blaine and Mr. Frelinghuysen have gone

[1] See *supra*, p. 41.   [2] See *supra*, p. 43.

to the extent of claiming their power to put aside the
stipulations of a treaty because it was found to oppose
their policy.[1] And more than this has taken place :
in their endeavours to emphasise their so-called right
of priority over the affairs of the American continent,
some statesmen have pushed the Doctrine, at times,
beyond any possibility of justification. Thus President
Hayes and Mr. Blaine went to the extent of proclaim-
ing that the canal should be "*virtually a part of the
coast-line of the United States.*"[2] Undoubtedly Lord
Granville was right in his opinion, and his remarks
were apposite, when he commented on the above
assertion in the following manner :—

"When the claim to do this (to fortify the canal
and obtain the exclusive control thereof) is accom-
panied by a declaration that the United States will
always insist on treating the waterway which shall
unite the two oceans 'as part of her coast-line,' it
is difficult to imagine that the States to which the
territory lying between that waterway and the United
States belongs, can practically retain as independent
a position as that which they now enjoy."[3]

We have also seen that, in 1903, before the Hay-
Bunau-Varilla treaty was signed, the administration
was considering a plan for submitting it to Congress,
whereby it would be proposed to disregard the inherent right of Colombia, the then sovereign of the
Isthmus of Panama, and proceed "to take what other
steps were needful in order to begin the enterprise."[4]

The examples of the policy of the United States
that have been thus recalled to the reader's mind

[1] See *supra*, pp. 46 et seq.   [2] See *supra*, pp. 40 and 43.
[3] *For. Rel.*, 1882, p. 302.   [4] See *supra*, p. 63.

would seem to be sufficient for establishing or invalidating the contention that the Monroe Doctrine is only the application of the right of self-preservation. The opinion prevails in Europe that the Doctrine is not a defensive measure, but rather an instrument for procuring the aggrandisement of the United States. The fact is, that the interests of the persons or countries engaged in the controversy are divergent, and hence it is difficult to reach a universal agreement upon the question.

From the limited scope of our inquiry it would not be difficult, however, to deduce that the Monroe Doctrine has been put forward on many occasions to justify measures which had nothing to do with preventing European interference in the American continent, but which, in fact, only tended to increase the power of the United States. The reason seems to be that from the beginning the Monroe Doctrine acquired a firm hold on the people, and is regarded with a kind of traditional reverence or sanctity. Politicians in the United States, well aware of this sentiment, have sometimes made the Doctrine serve their ends in their party politics, and thus it is that in the course of different administrations, and the consequent changes of opinion, it has been used at times as a defensive measure, while upon occasions it has been claimed to give the right for all sorts of aggression. In the opinion of Mr. J. B. Henderson[1] —and the course of events seems to justify his assertion—there is the danger that the more im-

[1] Mr. Henderson, an able American authority on the Monroe Doctrine, has dealt with the subject in a magisterial manner in his work entitled *American Diplomatic Questions*.

perialistic the United States becomes the more extended the Doctrine will be.

These amplifications of the Monroe Doctrine
that have been noticed are, together with the other
developments of the famous message, intimately
related to a factor of great importance that must not
be lost sight of, for it explains the connection, if any,
that exists between them and the original policy of
the United States. The extraordinary and inherent
flexibility or elasticity of the Doctrine is such, that
it has allowed, and will continue to allow, the government to make use of it under different sets of
circumstances, thus keeping pace with the enormous
and prodigious advancement of the nation. This
peculiarity of the Doctrine grants the government
special advantages, for they need not uphold it if in
the eyes of the administration it will not further
the interests of the United States, or in dubious
cases in which it is difficult of enforcement.

It must be borne in mind that the Monroe
Doctrine is not part of International Law. It is
merely the expression of the policy that the United
States will follow under certain circumstances. It
is true that the Latin American Republics have
accepted, and even have great reverence for, it but
only when applied in its original signification. It is
natural that these amplifications of the Doctrine that
tend to place the United States in a kind of patronis-
ing position with respect to the other states of the
New World, should be regarded with great distrust.
Of this hegemony that has been the offshot of the
Doctrine they are intensely suspicious. But even that
original part of the Doctrine that is approved by the

whole American continent cannot have a claim to be part of the law of nations. A state cannot issue rules for the regulation of international intercourse, unless all the other members of the family of nations accept such rules.

It may be remarked here that at the Hague Conference, 1899, the Doctrine was proclaimed *urbi et orbi* and in a solemn fashion by the delegates of the United States. They entered a reservation in signing the "Convention for the Peaceful Adjustment of International Differences," whereby they declared that "nothing contained in the convention shall be so construed as to require the United States of America to depart from its traditional policy of not entering upon, interfering with, or entangling itself in the political questions or internal administration of any foreign state, nor shall anything contained in the said convention be so construed as to require the relinquishment by the United States of America of its traditional attitude towards purely American questions."[1] This declaration was renewed on behalf of the United States at the Peace Conference of 1909. And Mr. Roosevelt, in his annual message to Congress in 1901, comments on the acceptance of such declaration by the Peace Conference of 1899 as an acquiescence of the powers there represented in the Monroe Doctrine.[2] But it must be pointed out that, although no protests against the conduct of the North American delegates was made, it is not to be supposed that the Doctrine thereby becomes law. Doctor Higgins, commenting on

[1] Cp. Holls, *The Peace Conference at the Hague*, pp. 267–272.
[2] Moore, *op. cit.* vol. vi. p. 594.

this fact, justly says that "it is difficult to see why the declaration of the United States delegate should be considered to have a bilateral effect, and the principle that 'silence gives consent' be invoked in so important a matter."[1] It is universally accepted, and rightly so, that the Doctrine belongs to the domain of politics and not to that of law.

From the foregoing brief sketch of the Monroe Doctrine, it becomes evident that the majority of the utterances of the Department of State in connection with trans-isthmian communication are devoid of *legal* force. But we have entered into a discussion of the views entertained by certain American statesmen, simply because they may serve as an indication of the ultimate results that may be reached in the subject of a canal across Central America. We have noted, on the one hand, the occasional endeavour of the United States to obtain the use of the waterway for their exclusive benefit as a development of the Monroe Doctrine; while, on the other hand, the interest taken by the other maritime powers, especially by Great Britain, in such communications has prompted them to attempt to counteract that tendency. To find out what has been the result of this controversy, that is to say, what legal principles will be made to apply to the Panama Canal, will be the subjuct of the succeeding chapters.

[1] Higgins, *The Hague Peace Conferences*, p. 174.

PART II.

THE JURIDICAL POSITION OF THE PANAMA CANAL.

CHAPTER I.

In entering into the foregoing historical sketch of the interoceanic canal question, it has been with the intention of discovering the different views that have obtained in connection with the status of this maritime communication. The political aspect of the subject only, therefore, has been studied. It is intended now to attempt the solution of the problem from a purely legal standpoint.

As both in the Hay-Pauncefote and in the Hay-Bunau-Varilla treaties the words "neutrality" and "neutralisation" are used with reference to the juridical position of the canal, it would be well to define as accurately as possible the meaning of these terms, so that we may be able to avoid the misconceptions and ambiguities that would naturally result if a different course were followed. If absolute truth were not necessarily to be attained in this way, we may at least circumscribe within narrow limits the many possibilities for error that are generally attendant on all questions in which technical terms play an important part.

Among the nations of old, belligerents never recognised an attitude of impartiality on the part of the states which had no active part in the hostilities. Some kind of assistance was always expected from those countries which were near the theatre of war; and if the expected aid was not forthcoming such states were regarded as actually hostile. But in the course of centuries a principle of impartiality on the part of those states foreign to the struggle has been developed, and to-day the body of rules which go to form that principle constitute one of the most important chapters of International Law. A state is, generally speaking, free to abstain from, or take part in, the hostilities when there is a state war; but if it chooses to abstain from acts of war it is said to be *neutral*, that is to say, that it takes no part in the contest and remains carrying on pacific intercourse with the belligerents. It follows, therefore, that the condition of neutrality in this sense can only exist in time of war, and applies only to those states which, of their own free will, abstain from taking part in the contest, observing thereby an attitude of impartiality towards the belligerents. But there are states and things, which have a neutral character, without having the option to join in the struggle or abstain from it.[1] These are neutralised states and neutralised things, and the process by which they have acquired this character is technically known as *Neutralisation*. Such states or things cannot have a belligerent nature. In the words of Professor Holland, "to neutralise is to bestow by convention a neutral character upon states, persons, and things which would or might otherwise bear a belligerent character."[2] As a

[1] Cp. Lawrence, *Essays on International Law*, pp. 143 et seq.
[2] *Fortnightly Review*, July 1883.

compensation for the obligation which they have of not taking part in warlike acts, a group of states protects them from all hostilities as long as they abide by their duty.

The practice of extending the principles of neutrality in this manner, and thus restricting the freedom of states, is of modern growth. The first example of any such process dates only to the last century. By a convention signed by Austria, France, Great Britain, Prussia, and Russia, on November 20, 1815, these powers declared their formal acknowledgment of the perpetual neutrality of Switzerland ; and they further guarantee to that country the integrity and inviolability of its territory. In 1839 the same powers and the Netherlands bestowed this status on Belgium. And in 1867 the Grand Duchy of Luxemburg, under the guarantees of Great Britain, Austria, France, Prussia, and Russia, was perpetually neutralised.

The reason why these states have acquired this peculiar condition has been undoubtedly a political one. The Great Powers have been anxious to uphold the balance of power in Europe, and in order to attain this end they have sought to preserve weak states between the territories of powerful nations, by covenanting that such weak states are not to be attacked, their territories becoming thereby free from the rigours of war. It has been necessary, therefore, in order that there should be a sanction sufficient to deter all aggression, that the agreement providing for neutralisation should be entered into by nations whose location gave them an interest in the question, and whose strength was such as to make effective the inviolability of the provisions contained in the convention. Although distant nations have not taken part in these arrangements, the facts that the guarantee of neutrality is perfectly effective and that so far the inviolability of the states concerned has not been affected, would seem to be sufficient in themselves for considering the neutrality of Switzerland, Belgium, and Luxemburg as part and parcel of the public law of Europe.

The same machinery has been used to obtain a different end. The doctors and nurses in attendance on the sick and wounded in war, even when in the service of the enemy, are said to be neutralised according to the Geneva Convention, 1864, which has been signed by representatives of nearly all the civilised nations.[1] The reason is that states have recognised the advisability of letting such persons do their beneficent work in time of war without any discrimination whatever. The hospitals and ambulances of combatants were neutralised in a similar way.

There is another kind of neutralisation, namely, that of certain portions of land or water for the purpose of excluding such places as parts of the regions of war. Primarily the territory of the belligerents and the open sea may be converted into the scene of battle, but the neutral character may be impressed on certain portions, and then no acts of war can be committed there. At present no part of the open sea is neutralised, but formerly the Black Sea was supposed to enjoy this status by virtue of the treaty

---

[1] It is to be observed that the term "neutrality" does not appear in the revised Geneva Convention of 1906. It is simply stated that the *personnel* engaged in the treatment of the wounded and the sick "shall be respected and protected under all circumstances" (Higgins, *op. cit.* p. 23).

of Paris, 1856, concluded by Great Britain, Austria, France, Prussia, Russia, Sardinia, and Turkey. It is not necessary here to enter into a discussion of the causes that led the powers to veil under the euphemism of neutrality the restriction imposed on Russia. But by the Treaty of London, 1871, freedom of action in the waters of the Black Sea was restored.

Savoy and the Ionian Islands of Corfu and Paxo are under an anomalous position, for, although they form part of unneutralised states, they are said to be endowed with the neutral character as a result of the agreements of the Great Powers.[1]

A conspicuous example of the neutralisation of a waterway may be found in the convention respecting the free navigation of the Suez Canal, 1888, entered into by all the Great Powers, and Holland, Spain, and Turkey. The ostensible and real object for adopting this line of action in this case has been to establish "a definite system destined to guarantee at all times, and for all the powers, the free use" of the waterway.[2]

The Republics of Argentine and Chile, in the same way, have wished to establish free navigation to the flags of all nations in the Straits of Magellan. To attain this object they have attempted to bestow upon the Straits the neutral character by providing in their treaty of July 1881 that they "are neutralised for ever."

[1] For a lucid discussion of the difficulties attendant on these cases in the event of a war of the powers affected, see Lawrence, *Principles of International Law*, 4th ed. pp. 601 et seq.

[2] For reasons which will subsequently appear, we content ourselves with this simple statement in this connection; but the discussion of the neutralisation of the Seuz Canal will be taken up later on, as, in our opinion, it affords a close parallel to the Panama Canal looked at from the legal standpoint.

The examination of the most important examples of neutralisation which have ever been effected will necessarily bear out the contention that a neutralised region will not be clothed with the belligerent character which it might normally have in time of war, were it not for the agreement between nations that it is to be endowed with the priviliges and obligations of neutrality. If the neutralised region constitutes a state, it is interdicted from making war, and all other states are forbidden from violating its neutral position. When doctors and nurses have a neutral character, it is intended that they should carry on their humane avocation without the interference to which they would be subjected if they were to be considered as belligerents. If portions of the sea or the land forming part of a state bear this character, the object sought is to restrict the right of a belligerent by preventing him from using such parts as the theatre of war. The peculiar interests of the maritime nations of the world in certain passages connecting two open seas has brought about the neutralisation of waterways so as to insure freedom of passage. And this freedom of transit would extend to the innocent passage of warships in time of war as well as in time of peace. We see, therefore, that the same means has been adopted for different ends. The reason is that a necessary consequence of the process of neutralisation is always common to all the cases—freedom from hostilities—even though the objects which it is intended to establish may be and are utterly unlike.

Neutralisation is a principle of International Law. Hence it is evident that in order to obtain neutralisation it is necessary that there should be actual or tacit consent on the part of the members of the family of nations to respect the principles embodied in the notion. International Law, springing as it does from the *consensus* of nations, and Neutralisation being of modern growth, it necessarily follows that an act or agreement is essential in order to establish the rights and duties created. Although the theory of the Equality of states holds good, yet it is not possible that *universal* assent should be demanded in order to consider that a given change in International relations is to be deemed as forming part of the general law of Nations. The formal act or agreement establishing the neutralisation of a given thing need not necessarily be subscribed by absolutely all the civilised nations of the globe, but it is submitted that such a number of states must be parties to the act as to ensure its enforcement against others. Yet it is quite possible that the engagement need not be entered into by a sufficiently large number of states to make the guarantee effective, if there is a tacit understanding among the majority of states that points unequivocally to the conclusion that they will respect such neutrality, and, if the case should ever occur, be willing to prevent its infringement. It is therefore with truth that it has been suggested that the successful application of neutralisation depends "upon the existence of a state of mind among the rulers and peoples concerned, which shall make them willing not only to respect the guarantee of neutrality themselves, but also to enforce it against others."[1]

Neutralisation which has not been established in

[1] Lawrence, *op. cit.* 3rd ed. p. 466.

this way cannot be said to have any legal force.
The rights which states have *inter se* would be
necessarily altered by the process, and hence they
cannot be restricted without their consent. A state
is unable by its sole declaration to impose the
obligation on other states to respect its neutrality by
the mere fact that it has decreed that its territory or
part of it is to be neutralised. In 1856 the Khedive
declared that the Suez Canal and its ports should be
considered as neutral. But this unilateral statement
was not regarded as sufficient to render the seizure
of the canal by Great Britain in 1882 an offence
against the law of the civilised world.

In dealing with the important subject of a
unilateral declaration of neutralisation, we must be
careful in our way of reasoning so as to avoid a
confusion between the political and the juridical view
of the question. In order to obtain cogency and
precision in our conclusions, let us examine the
opinion of M. F. de Martens, the learned Russian
Professor. He considers that the view taken by the
majority of international jurists to the effect that an
act of neutralisation must necessarily be signed and
approved by the Great Powers is absolutely inadmissible. He goes on to observe that in private life
nobody contests our right to declare once for all that
it is our intention to keep a perfect neutrality in the
quarrels of our neighbours and acquaintances; that,
therefore, in the political or international life, the
same right should be recognised to states so that
they may declare *urbi et orbi*, and for all time, that
they have decided to remain out of all international
complications and will not take part in the conflicts

arising between nations.[1] Now the premises of the famous jurist are perfectly sound, but the conclusion which he makes them to yield, we respectfully submit, is entirely false. True it is that a nation is at liberty to proclaim far and wide that she has decided to abstain from all international conflicts in the future ; nobody has suggested that Colombia or Egypt were committing a breach of law by declaring in their municipal regulations the " neutrality " of certain parts of their territories. The real, question is whether such unilateral declarations would have any *legal* force in International Law, so that other nations would respect, and abide by, the decision ; that is to say, whether the unilateral declaration would be sufficient to create an obligation in law. As no other seems to be the suggestion of the learned professor, we venture to subscribe our opinion in the negative for the following two reasons : (i) From the point of view of general jurisprudence nobody can impose on himself a legal obligation, for this would mean that he himself would seek its enforcement ; if he imposes it on himself he could also liberate himself from it at will, and hence it cannot be legally binding.[2] (ii) A state cannot impose on others an obligation without their consent. This would be against the very nature of International Law.[3]

For identical reasons we feel compelled to dissent also from the view of M. Descamps.[4] He equally

---

[1] F. de Martens, " La Neutralisation du Danemark," *Revue des Deux Mondes*, Nov. 15, 1903.

[2] See Austin's *Lectures on Jurisprudence*, 11th ed. p. 192.

[3] See *supra*, pp. 89, 90.

[4] *La Neutralité de la Belgique. Étude sur la constitution des États pacifiques à titre permanente*, 1902, pp. 304 et seq.

suggests the existence of a "*neutralité permanente érigée en maxime d'État.*" This view, as has been pointed out by M. Hagerup,[1] partakes more of a political than of a juridical conception. Similarly two or three states are incapable of effecting the neutralisation of a certain area. In view of this, we venture to suggest that the provision of the treaty between Argentine and Chile, 1882, providing for the neutralisation of the Straits of Magellan, has not in itself any validity in International Law so as to constitute any interference with it an offence against the public law of nations. If there exists a tacit understanding on the part of the more important maritime nations to respect and uphold the engagement, then and then only can the Magellan's Straits be deemed to have a definite status in International Law. But as long as there is no evidence in this direction, any nation at war with either of the contracting parties would be absolutely free to disregard the declaration.

It would seem perfectly clear from the succinct analysis which has been made, that although neutralisation cannot be said to have arrived at its final stage on account of the comparatively short time that has elapsed since the first attempt to neutralise, yet the process undoubtedly establishes a definite status for the states, persons, or things on which the neutral character is bestowed. As soon as this status has been properly apprehended the difficulties and intricacies of the subject would be diminished when it is sought to discover whether a given object bears that character. It is possible that

---

[1] *La Neutralité permanente*, 1905.

an imperfect apprehension of the true meaning of the notion may lead diplomatists to use the term as applied to certain things which, in fact, owing to the special circumstances of the case, do not bear that character. It is also conceivable, on the other hand, that the term may not be used in describing the international position of states, persons, or things, and yet there may be no doubt whatever that they have this particular status on account of the peculiar advantages and restrictions that have been granted and imposed, and also for the object that has been intended to secure.[1] It is then the business of the International lawyer to examine these cases under the light of legal theory, and discriminate between real and mistaken examples of neutralisation.

[1] Thus in the convention that definitely establishes the international position of the Suez Canal, the word neutralisation and its kindred terms do not appear, yet there cannot be any doubt as to the status of this waterway.

CHAPTER II.

GENERAL PRINCIPLES BEARING ON THE QUESTION
OF THE NEUTRALISATION OF WATERWAYS.

AFTER the brief examination of the theory of
neutralisation, it would be profitable to discuss certain
general principles applicable to artificial maritime
routes, so that we may be enabled to bring the
question of the Panama Canal under their light, and
then proceed to draw our inferences as free from
ambiguities and vagueness as it is possible. It has
been seen what neutralisation is, as well as the
purposes for which it is accomplished and the manner
of making it effective. But instead of proceeding
immediately to apply the principles thus observed
to the case of the interoceanic waterway, it might be
expedient to deal with other more specific factors
that are considered to bear an intimate relation to
the matter in hand, and which may greatly contribute
to explain the ultimate position which the canal is
made to assume.

It is hardly necessary to point out that maritime
problems are of transcendent value to all peoples.
If the sea is considered from the point of view of
serving as a highway between the different nations
of the globe, its great importance is immediately

realised.   It is to be remembered that the rule of the open sea was one of the first recognised principles of the law of nations, in spite of the fact that the existence of an international community was not clearly perceived at the beginnings of the science of International Law.   Interoceanic canals serve the same purpose, for they facilitate that intercourse that is essential for the relations of the different members of the family of nations.   And they not only have a commercial value, but they also play an important part from the political and strategic points of view, and are therefore of great importance in the hostile as well as in the peaceful intercourse of nations.

But it is only to those maritime routes that facilitate the means of communication between different nations, and which on this account can be termed of *general* interest, that the above remarks will apply.   For those artificial canals that only or mainly serve the purpose of the state through which they pass, can have no claim to such international importance.   The former may ultimately be considered to be under the domain of International Law, all nations having equal rights on them ; while the latter would be governed by the municipal regulations of the power concerned, and would be, therefore, under their exclusive control.

In spite of the great importance that these artificial canals have, they are the result of recent development.   It is only during comparatively late years that men have realised the expediency of obtaining direct and prompt means of communication; and even if the want of them had been felt before, there were insurmountable difficulties for carrying a projected enterprise to a successful termination. It is then on account of the novelty of the enterprise that so many difficulties may be encountered in ascertaining positively the juridical status of these artificial highways. When a new problem is set for solution, human ingenuity is immediately directed by a natural process to find the relation that may exist between the new facts and some other problem whose solution has already been established. Thus it is that in the case of artificial canals attempts have been made to show that there is a real analogy between them and the ordinary straits that connect two seas, on the one hand, and the territorial waters of the state or states through which the canal is made, on the other.

It is asserted by some writers that interoceanic canals become, on account both of their very nature and of the purposes for which they are made, integral parts of the open sea, on the same footing as natural straits, and should therefore be always free to the passage of all vessels, that is to say, that they should never be closed to the war flag of a belligerent.[1]

In opposition to this view, it is contended that the piercing of a canal does not thereby denationalise the territory through which it passes ; the conclusion drawn from this being that artificial waterways should not be assimilated to natural straits but to the territorial waters of the respective states.[2]

This latter opinion is again opposed on the ground

[1] See Calvo, *Le Droit international theorique et pratique*, t. i. p. 507. The delegate of Austria-Hungary to the Conference of Paris (1885) expressed the view that there was a real analogy between artificial canals and natural straits.

[2] Rossignol, *Le Canal de Suez*, pp. 166 et seq.

of drawing from the premises an inexact conclusion. For, it is said, in the ports and bays of a neutral state belligerent vessels remain *stationary*, while in maritime canals they are *moving*, for their object is merely to cross its waters.[1]

A further suggestion is possible, which, from one point of view, has the advantage of reconciling the assimilation of canals to territorial waters with the above objection. It consists in the claim that all the rules relative to rivers must analogously be applied to canals.[2]

It will perhaps be apposite to remark here that questions of analogy are extremely difficult, and it follows that if the essential characteristics of the notion have not been fully grasped the logical deductions that the argument is made to yield would necessarily contain misleading, if not entirely erroneous, conclusions. It seems clear to us that the fact of these canals being artificial is an important characteristic, and must cause, therefore, all the foregoing analogies to break down.

The objection might be raised that such canals seem to be parts of the territories of the respective states because they have been before integral parts thereof, and could only come into existence through their assent and acquiescence. For, *prima facie*, a state is free to do with its property anything that it deems fit, and is consequently at liberty to cause

---

[1] Cp. Abribat, *Le Détroit de Magellan au point de vue international*, 1902, p. 211.

[2] Much valuable information on the subject of canals may be found in Oppenheim, *International Law*, vol. i. p. 233 ; Holland, *Studies*, pp. 270-298 ; Bustamante, "Le Canal de Panama et le Droit International," *Revue de Droit International*, tome 27, pp. 223 and 227.

7

canals to be opened in its territories, such canals to be under its exclusive control and regulation, so that no other states would have a right, apart from special conventions, to the advantages that may be derived from the new route. But, on the other hand, it must be borne in mind that there exist in International Law some well-established principles as regards the freedom of passage by what may be considered to be the world's thoroughfares that tend to indicate that, when a certain route has been opened for *international purposes*, the territorial state through which that route passes—and indeed any other state that may have a special interest in it—is expected to relinquish, to a certain extent, its jurisdiction. The stretch of land or water thus affected ceases to be, from the international standpoint, governed by the national law of that state, and passes to the domain of the law of nations. In fact, the route becomes international because it is dedicated to the use of all nations, that is, on account of its international object —a result that is always due to the peculiar position of the place in question. When this is the case it may be a question, at least in theory, whether a state by altering the world's thoroughfares is not thereby producing material changes that would have peculiar effects in the development of other countries, and these effects may, potentially at least, bring about a certain amount of evil in the relations of other countries. Under these circumstances one would then feel inclined to suggest that a state cannot, without the acquiescence of the other parties interested, proceed to open a canal of communication, for it may influence their future destinies. But of course states readily acquiesce in cases of this nature, provided that such canals should be governed by International Law, for in this way there would be ample assurance that they would be used for the benefit of all the parties interested. This doctrine would be only the application of the juridical maxim of *sic utere tuo ut alienum non lædas*, which, in turn, is derived from a principle of general jurisprudence that goes to show the inadvisability of pushing abstract principle to its logical results, when it is intended to deal with practical problems—*summum jus summa injuria.*

The fact seems to be that the question is *sui generis*, and cannot, therefore, be solved by reference to existing notions. The legal position of these artificial canals cannot be ascertained by using ana-logical arguments. The diplomatic history of the Suez and Panama Canals has amply shown this fact. The negotiations, disagreements, delays, and doubts, all go to prove the veracity of the assertion. But this does not mean, of course, that certain general principles of International Law would be absolutely unavailable in determining the status of these water-ways. Primarily it is a matter for special conventions, but the principles to which reference has been made would greatly contribute to decide the question.

It further remains to be noticed in this connection, that it seems obvious that the ultimate status which would be given to waterways of this nature cannot in any way be affected by the fact that the canal is constructed by a government or by private enterprise. That is to say, the public or private nature of the undertaking is by no means a material point in determining its position in International Law. And the reasons for this fact are not difficult to find. It is of course the individual who first perceives the necessity or the expediency of helping human development. But the activities of the modern state are so varied and complex, and may be traced to such very different sources, that it would be idle to speculate upon them in this connection. It may be pointed out, however, that economical or political reasons may prompt a state to take in hand the accomplishment of a given task without there existing any real difference in its results when the matter is dealt with from a juridical point of view.

The Panama Canal, it is well known, was taken up for construction by the United States as a government enterprise, on account of the generally accepted belief that private capital could not command sufficient resources for the completion of such an enormous work.[1]

Another point that seems to be equally ineffectual in determining the legal position of the waterway is the fact that the canal is constructed in territory that does not belong to the nation engaged in the opera-

[1] Mr. Roosevelt summarises thus one of the reasons why the United States undertook the completion of the Panama Canal: "It is not worth while belonging to a big nation unless the big nation is willing when the necessity arises to undertake a big task. . . . When we acquired the right to build the Panama Canal, and entered on the task, there were worthy people who came to me, and said they wondered whether it would pay. I always answered that it was one of the great world works which had to be done ; that it was our business as a nation to do it, if we were really to make good our claim to be treated as a great world power; and that as we were unwilling to abandon the claim, no American worth his salt ought to hesitate about performing the task." (Speech of Mr. Roosevelt delivered at the Mansion House, *The Times*, June 1, 1910.)

tion. If this fact has any importance at all from the international standpoint, it is in showing that the general interest awakened with reference to the question is such that it has attracted foreign activity on account of the national resources being too poor for the magnitude of the work undertaken.

Finally, it may be submitted that the two last facts discussed—that is, the governmental character of the enterprise and the actual carrying out of the plans in foreign territory—may in some way influence the political history of the waterway, but with regard to its legal position they afford no clue, especially when there exist conventional agreements that purport to define its status.

CHAPTER III.

FACTORS THAT CONTRIBUTE TO GIVE TO THE PANAMA
CANAL AN INTERNATIONAL STATUS.

IT has been hinted at, though not expressly stated, that the neutralisation attached to a certain region, when considered apart from conventional agreements, mainly depends on the following three facts :[1]—

    I. *The geographical position of the place in question ;*

    II. *Its history,* and

    III. *The interest that the world at large may have in it.*

It is clear, however, that these questions, which we now consider as separate from each other, are not really so from a different point of view, for one of them may at once depend on, or result from, the others. Thus the geographical position that a certain place occupies may account for its history and for the special interest that mankind takes in it, and the result of this interest may be reflected in the conventional agreements of certain nations. But it will be convenient for our purpose to deal with them separately. The above facts will be discussed in their order.

[1] Cp. Martens, *op. cit.* and *loc. cit.*

I. Geographical Position of the Panama Canal.

It is well known that the canal is being built in the narrowest stretch of land—less than fifty miles wide—that connects North and South America. It is, therefore, hardly necessary to enter here into a long description of its geographical peculiarities in order to emphasise the importance of the route, not only from the economical, but also from the political and strategical standpoints. The canal when terminated will be in the nature of an artificial strait connecting the two great oceans. Its position is such that it will necessarily alter the international thoroughfares.

It is not intended, nor will it be relevant to the subject, to enter here into a detailed and accurate account of the extent to which the Panama Canal will shift the centre of gravity in relation to the world routes, or what will be the advantages that the artificial waterway will have over the natural or actual condition of things. But some remarks on the subject will be germane to the present inquiry. It is obvious that the route between New Zealand and European countries on the Atlantic will be appreciably shortened. Japan, Australia, and New Zealand will be within more easy reach of the ports on the Atlantic coast of the American continent. Thus the new canal will make the travelling distance by sea between New York and Yokohama some 3400 miles less than under present conditions. There will also be a comparatively rapid maritime communication between Europe and the Pacific states of the New

World, as well as between the latter and those on the Atlantic littoral.

These are the main points to be considered in dealing with the extraordinary possibilities and opportunities that will be brought into being by the opening of the canal. It is possible, indeed probable, that a host of problems of a commercial, political, or strategical nature will be created that will not fail to affect a large number of the members of the international family.

II. History of the Panama Canal.

It will not be necessary to repeat here what has been said in this connection when dealing with the policy of the United States towards the canal question. Throughout the whole history of trans-isthmian communication in the New World we can see that the territorial power has never intended to make of the canal a monopoly. If this could bring some advantages, the disadvantages and the difficulties that it would entail would be so great that in fact it would not be worth while to attempt it. Other nations have not been slow in recognising this fact; hence it is that, as has been remarked by Professor Latané, all the arrangements in reference to the canal contemplate some sort of neutralisation.[1] As early as 1866, New Granada, to which power then belonged the territory through which the canal was to be constructed, passed a law declaring the perpetual neutrality of the ports at each end of the canal and of its waters. In 1875 another law was passed for the same

[1] *Op. cit.* and *loc. cit.*; cp. also pp. 13, 16, 18, 28, 30, 37, *supra.*

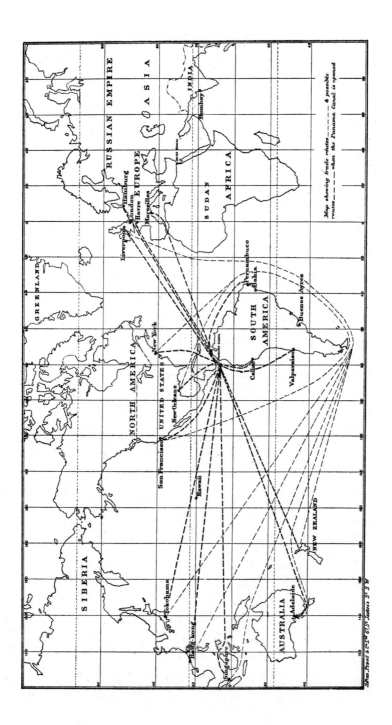

Map showing trade routes ——— A possible
routes —-—-— when the Panama Canal is opened

SIBERIA

GREENLAND

RUSSIAN EMPIRE

ASIA

INDIA

Bombay

London
Hamburg
Havre
EUROPE
Marseilles

Liverpool

SUDAN

AFRICA

NORTH AMERICA

New York

UNITED STATES

New Orleans

San Francisco

Hawaii

PANAMA CANAL

SOUTH
AMERICA

Callao

Pernambuco
Bahia

Buenos Ayres

Valparaiso

Yokohama

Hong Kong

Singapore

NEW ZEALAND

AUSTRALIA

Adelaide

Edwa Weed & C.ⁱᵈ 67,S⁴ James's St S W

purpose.[1] Although it has been stated already, we may remind the reader of the proposition of Spain to obtain passage for her troops and munitions of war across the Isthmus of Panama at the time of her war with Peru. The United States proposed to refuse the transit in virtue of their treaty with New Granada, 1846. Had the canal then been built, and if the theory that the neutralisation of a waterway, in contraposition to the neutralisation of territory, meant freedom of passage at all times had become current, it is evident that the decision of the Attorney-General of the United States would have been entirely different.

In short, we may say that the whole history of interoceanic communication in the New World, during the last century, points unequivocally to the conclusion

---

[1] Perhaps it may be interesting to quote here the words of the provision : " The government of the Republic declares the waters of the canal, from ocean to ocean, as well as the ports at its termini, neutral for all time. Consequently, in case of war between other nations or between one of them and New Granada, the canal transit shall not be interrupted thereby. All merchant vessels or citizens of any nation of the world may enter and cross the canal without molestation or detention ; provided that no foreign troops be permitted to pass without the permission of Congress. The entrance to or transit of the canal shall be most rigorously prohibited to the war vessels of a belligerent " (Arts. 10 and 11 of the New Granadian Law of June 27, 1866). It will be noticed that "neutrality" is taken to mean the absence of all kinds of war implements in the canal. We need not be surprised at the prohibition for war vessels to pass through the canal. It has only been in the course of the last few years that the essential characteristic in the neutralisation of a waterway (different from the case of neutralisation of land) is taken to mean *freedom of transit in time of peace as well as in time of war.* Thus it is that some writers still assert, quite mistakenly, that the Suez Canal is not neutralised *because vessels of war would be allowed to pass.* (Cp. Abribat, *Le Détroit de Magellan au point de vue international*, p. 236 ; Bonfils, *Manuel de Droit international public*, p. 296 ; Westlake, *International Law*, Part I. p. 330.)

that the Panama Canal should be open and free to all the nations of the world under equal terms, and that this opinion has been repeatedly uttered not only by the leading statesmen of Europe and South America, but also by nearly all the North American Presidents and their Secretaries of State.[1] It is true that President Hayes, Mr. Evarts, Mr. Blaine, and Mr. Frelinghuysen used language that implied a limited and restricted use of the canal by other powers, according to the wishes, and for the main, if not the exclusive, advantage of the United States;[2] but it must be remembered that this later policy was the issue of an aggressive and imperialist tendency on the part of the United States, and has never been accepted by the other maritime powers. We have had already occasion to notice the remarks of Mr. Blaine and Mr. Frelinghuysen, and if something more should be added to what we then said, it would be to the effect that their reasoning was defective, to say the least, for it proved to be devoid of legal and moral support not less than of comity.

It is possible that some manifestations tending in the same direction may have been indulged in by other North American politicians, but these may have been inspired by the strong disapproval which they felt for the provisions of the Clayton-Bulwer treaty that condemned them to inaction on the subject of canal communication across Central America; and such tendencies may now be considered as entirely non-existent by the effect of the Hay-Pauncefote Convention.

[1] See *supra*, *e.g.* pp. 11, 13, 15, 18, 20, 24, 28, 50, and 53.
[2] See *supra*, pp. 40, 43 et seq.

III. THE INTERNATIONAL INTEREST IN THE QUESTION OF THE PANAMA CANAL.

The interest that the world at large has in the subject of a maritime communication between the Atlantic and the Pacific is so patent that there is no need to insist on the question. M. de Lesseps well perceived this fact, and it alone explains his exertions in this connection. He regarded the work of Panama in the same plane as that of Suez; for this reason he conceived the idea of extending to the canal and its approaches the privileges of neutrality. Holland had already launched a project for the construction of this work, and later Bonaparte took steps in the same direction. The question has been more than once raised in England, and although it proved abortive she has never lost sight of the importance of the subject. Her interest is well evidenced by the treaties concluded with the United States and some of the Central American Republics in this respect. She has even been on the verge of war to uphold her contentions in connection with the interoceanic communication.

The Latin American States, although always suspicious of the influence that the United States may exert on them, have expressed the interest which they feel in the construction of the canal. At the second International Conference of American States held at Mexico, 1901–2, they unanimously adopted a resolution declaring that this work would be "in the highest sense a work of civilisation, and to the greatest degree beneficial to the development of commerce between the American States and the other countries of the world."

The above examination of the principal factors, apart from conventional agreements, clearly demonstrates that the position of the Panama Canal is one that cannot be defined by the mere will of a single nation. The international interests at stake are so many and so important, that it is imperative that in deciding the ultimate status that the canal will be made to assume, account should be taken of this plurality of interests, so that the result achieved should be both equitable and productive of welfare and advancement for mankind. It is, then, on account of the existence of all the different circumstances that have been described, that a formal and solemn treaty has been entered into, by means of which it is intended to devote the Panama Canal to the unrestricted use of all nations at all times.

CHAPTER IV.

CONVENTIONAL AGREEMENTS PROVIDING FOR THE NEUTRALISATION OF THE PANAMA CANAL.

THE treaties that exist on the subject have been mentioned more than once, but the validity, strength, and meaning of their provisions have not as yet been subjected to a severe analysis.

The preamble of the Hay-Pauncefote treaty states that both Great Britain and the United States are desirous to facilitate the construction of an inter-oceanic canal, "and to that end to remove any objection which may arise out of the convention of the 19th of April 1850, commonly called the Clayton-Bulwer treaty, to the construction of such canal under the auspices of the government of the United States, *without impairing the general principle of neutralisation established in Article VIII. of that Convention,*[1] have for that purpose," etc.

It follows from this, as has been ably remarked,[2] that Great Britain and the United States have recognised, first, that a "general principle" of neutralisation has been established by Article VIII. of the

---

[1] The italics are our own.
[2] Peter C. Hains, "The Neutralisation of the Panama Canal," *American Journal of International Law*, April 1909.

Clayton-Bulwer treaty, and secondly, that such principle is not impaired by the Hay-Pauncefote Convention.

The "general principle" of neutralisation referred to is then contained in the Clayton-Bulwer treaty, and, as we have already observed,[1] is to the effect that (*a*) in case of war between the contracting parties, their vessels traversing the canal shall be exempted from blockade, detention, or capture (Art. II.); (*b*) the persons employed in making the said canal, and their property used for that object, are to be protected from unjust detention, confiscation, seizure, or any violence whatever (Art. III.); and (*c*) the contracting parties are bound to protect the canal from interruption, seizure, or unjust confiscation, and they "*guarantee the neutrality thereof, so that the said canal may be open and free.*"[2]

We hold that the foregoing provisions go to form the so-called "general principle" of neutralisation spoken of. It is true that the Hay-Pauncefote treaty mentions only Article VIII. of the Clayton-Bulwer, and that this article speaks merely of extending the "protection" of the contracting powers to any practicable communication; but the whole tenor of the article clearly shows that its meaning and application cannot be ascertained otherwise than by reference to all the other articles of that treaty. The wording of Article VIII. is such that it leaves no doubt whatever as to what was intended. It begins by saying that "the governments of the United States and Great Britain having not only desired, in entering into this Convention, to accomplish a par-

[1] See *supra*, p. 31.   [2] The italics are the author's.

ticular object, but also to establish a general principle, they hereby agree to extend their protection by treaty stipulations," etc.   What is this "*general principle*"? How else can it be ascertained than by reference to the other articles of the treaty?   It is evident that the "protection" spoken of is a wide one.   Besides, if "*the general principle*" of which the article speaks meant a mere protection, why should Great Britain and the United States refer to it as "the general principle" *of neutralisation*? Surely the presence of the last two words is full of meaning.

This "general principle" of neutralisation, then, which is not impaired by the Hay-Pauncefote treaty, provides for the freedom of transit, the immunity of the canal from hostilities, and the protection of the works.   So far the intention of the contracting parties in 1850 and in 1901 seems to be perfectly clear.   The treaty of 1850 is superseded, not abrogated.   The provisions that conflict with the new arrangements cease to be of any effect, but those parts in which no conflict occurs are perfectly binding. The main object of the Hay-Pauncefote treaty was to do away with the estoppel that had been created by the convention of 1850.   It will be remembered that by the latter convention neither of the contracting parties could acquire an exclusive control over the route.   The treaty of 1901 provides that the canal may be constructed under the auspices of the government of the United States, and thereby removes the objection which arose out of the Clayton-Bulwer Convention.

Let us now examine the further internal evidence

that may exist in the Hay-Pauncefote treaty with regard to the international position of the Panama Canal. In its Article III. direct reference is made to the neutralisation of the Suez Canal. The United States expressly adopts some rules substantially embodied in the Convention of Constantinople, 1888, to govern the position of the Panama Canal. Now it is hardly necessary to enter into a discussion as to whether the Suez Canal is neutralised or not, for there is no doubt whatever as to the international status of this waterway. Why should the essential characteristics of neutralisation be drawn from the convention that in fact establishes the neutrality of the Suez Canal and make them applicable to the interoceanic route, if it had not been intended that the Panama Canal should be in the same position?

The declaratory provisions of the Hay-Pauncefote treaty may be summarised as follows :—

I. The canal shall be free and open to ships of war and merchantmen of all nations observing these rules, on terms of absolute equality.

II. The canal shall never be blockaded, nor shall any right of war or act of hostility be committed within it.

III. Belligerent vessels shall not revictual or take any stores in the canal, except when it is strictly necessary.

IV. Belligerent vessels shall cross the canal with the least possible delay. Prizes shall be in all respects subject to the same rules as vessels of war.

V. "No belligerent shall embark or disembark troops, munitions of war, or warlike materials in the canal except in case of accidental hindrance of the transit."

VI. All the above provisions shall apply to waters adjacent to the canal, within three marine miles of either end. Belligerent vessels shall not remain in such waters longer than twenty-four hours at any one time, except in cases of distress.

VII. But a vessel of war of one belligerent shall not be allowed to depart within twenty-four hours from the departure of a vessel of war of the other belligerent.

VIII. All works necessary to the construction and maintenance of the canal shall enjoy complete immunity from attack or injury by belligerents.

IX. "It is agreed that no change of territorial sovereignty or of the international relations of the countries or country traversed by the before-mentioned canal shall affect the general principle of neutralisation or the obligation of the high contracting parties under the present treaty." [1]

It is only fair to make a few observations on these provisions before dealing with other matters. In the Hay-Pauncefote treaty it is said that the United States "adopts" those rules as the basis of neutralisation, instead of providing that both the high contracting parties agree to be governed by them. On this account it seems to have been suggested that the United States would be free to disregard them at any time that they might think it fit. This is undoubtedly a mistaken view; the article referred to is unilateral in appearance only; it is enough to read Article II. of the same treaty in order to see the real spirit of the whole convention. "It is agreed," runs the article, "that . . . *subject to the provisions of the present treaty*," [2] the United States shall have and enjoy all the rights incident to such construction. The article

---

[1] In the wording of this article, which has been transcribed here *verbatim*, a further indication as to the intention of the contracting parties may be found. They say in an unequivocal manner that certain changes shall not "affect *the general principle of neutralisation or the obligation of the high contracting parties under the present treaty.*" They had a definite and clear conception as to the "general principle of neutralisation," and to this conception, which they did not want to impair, the further obligations of the Hay-Pauncefote treaty were added.

[2] The italics are our own.

8

dealing with the neutralisation of the canal contains some of the provisions referred to. It follows, therefore, that they are binding on the United States as much as any other engagement of the same treaty.

Reference may also be made to the fact that in the Hay-Pauncefote convention it is said that "the canal shall be free and open to the vessels of commerce and of war of all nations observing these rules," whereas in the corresponding provision applicable to the Suez Canal, the words "always" and "in time of peace as in time of war" are to be found. It is thought by some that the absence of these words is very suggestive, and they seem to take it to signify that the United States may close the canal to belligerents or to a power that is at war with her. But one needs only to read the rules relating to belligerents to see that free transit of vessels of war is guaranteed, and this free transit extends, by implication, to the vessels of a potential enemy of the United States. It may be allowed to remind the reader that in the original treaty signed by Mr. Hay and Lord Pauncefote, February 5, 1900, which had been ratified by the Senate, with some amendments which the British Government did not accept, the rule runs to the effect that "the canal shall be free and open, *in time of war as in time of peace.*" The Senate never objected to the wording of the provision in this manner.[1] Possibly on account of its redundance, for its meaning can be obtained from the context, it disappeared from the newer draft.

With regard to the suggestion that passage through the canal may be refused to an enemy of

[1] Cp. Moore, *A Digest of International Law*, vol. iii. pp. 210 and 211.

the United States, it may be profitable to remark that by one of the amendments suggested by the Senate, it was proposed to enact that none of the rules relating to the neutralisation of the canal "*shall apply to measures which the United States may find it necessary to take for securing by its own forces the defence of the United States and the maintenance of public order.*"[1] The British Government repudiated this provison, and, in consequence, it does not appear in the finally accepted treaty. On the contrary, there is a general provision in imperative language prohibiting that "any right of war be exercised or any act of hostility be committed" within the canal. And the universal application of this prohibition is further emphasised by showing that it is intended to apply to the United States themselves, for the provision is followed by a *restricted* relaxation in favour of this power in the following terms: "The United States, *however*, shall be at liberty to maintain such military police along the canal as may be necessary to protect it against lawlessness and disorder."[2]

We may now pass to deal with another treaty that has some direct reference to the position of the Panama Canal. This is the so-called Hay-Bunau-Varilla Convention. Its main purpose, and the circumstances under which it was entered into, have already been mentioned. It only remains for us, therefore, to consider those provisions that have a direct application to the point now at issue.

---

[1] Cp. Moore, *A Digest of International Law*, vol. iii. pp. 210 and 211.
[2] The emphasis of this sentence is clearly in the word "however," and for this reason we have put it in italics.

In the Hay-Bunau-Varilla treaty, 1903, concluded between the United States and the Republic of Panama, it is provided that the canal shall be opened upon the terms of, and in conformity with, all the stipulations of the Hay-Pauncefote Convention. But the treaty is not satisfied with this reference to the position that the canal would be made to assume. It goes on, therefore, to state in express terms that "the canal, when constructed, and the entrances thereto shall be neutral in perpetuity."[1] And, again, further reference is made to the international position of the waterway in the following terms: "For the better performance of the engagements of this convention, and to the end of the efficient protection of the canal and the *preservation of its neutrality*, the government of the Republic of Panama will sell. . . . ."[2] It would be nothing less than a patent misrepresentation of the meaning of words to say that something in the nature of a neutralised status was not intended to be bestowed on the canal. And in order to emphasise further the right of free transit, it is agreed that the government of the Republic of Panama "shall have the right to transport over the canal its vessels and its troops and munitions of war in such vessels at all times."[3]

It is evident that the above engagements reflect the intention of the United States, and are in harmony with the provisions of the Hay-Pauncefote treaty, which was expressly mentioned in this connection.[4] On the other hand, the national interests of the Republic of Panama are so vitally dependent

[1] Article XVIII.   [2] Article XXV.
[3] Article XIX.   [4] Article XVIII.

on the question, that she could not help being intensely apprehensive of the ultimate position in which the canal would be placed. Any one can see that it would have been utter ruin for her even to consider the possibility of the construction of the canal across her territory, if she did not feel assured that the route would be clothed with the privileges of neutrality. How could she escape the dangers of a great war, to which she was not a party, if hostilities could be carried on in the canal or its approaches?

The simple truth is, that when she entered into the necessary stipulations, it was understood that the canal would be free from hostilities even in the case of a war to which the United States was a party. For "the land on which the canal is being built," in the words of an American writer, "was conveyed to the United States for a special purpose, and is held *in trust* to secure the execution of that purpose." [1]

[1] Col. Peter C. Hains, *op. cit.* and *loc. cit.* p. 373.

CHAPTER V.

THE Suez Canal affords the only precedent that exists in International Law in relation to the neutralisation of artificial waterways. For this reason, and also because the Hay-Pauncefote treaty avowedly adopts the Convention of Constantinople as its model, it would seem advisable to inquire into the relative positions of the two canals, so as to ascertain in a clear manner whether a real analogy exists between them, and, if that is the case, to proceed to strengthen the conclusions which have already been hinted at as the result of our arguments from general principles and from the provisions contained in the treaty that regulates the status of the Panama Canal. It will be seen, therefore, that it is not absolutely essential for our purpose to draw out the possible parallelism that may exist between the positions of the Suez and Panama Canals. But the inquiry would be, nevertheless, interesting and profitable.

Let us then proceed with those points in which the two canals have a well-marked similarity :—

[1] An interesting account on this subject can be obtained in Woolsey, "Suez and Panama—A Parallel," in *Annual Report of the American Historical Association*, 1902. Cp. also Bustamante, *op. cit.* and *loc. cit.*

I. Either of them is in the nature of an artificial strait connecting two seas, their geographical conditions having been identical.

II. Each canal lies wholly within the territory of a single power.

III. The territorial powers under whose sovereignty the canals are placed are both too poor to finance the enterprise and too weak to protect the works when terminated.

IV. They equally resemble one another in the fact that in each case foreign capital has been sought and obtained in order to bring the undertaking to a successful issue.

V. If an inquiry is made into the respective histories of these waterways, facts of striking similarity will be discovered. There we shall find that the various endeavours to save time in navigation are not different in any essential points. In the same manner, the territorial powers have felt exactly corresponding fears as to the future position of their canals; thus the Sublime Porte by firmans of 1856 and 1866, and New Granada by her laws of 1866 and 1875, proclaimed their respective zones of land through which the canals were to pass to be neutral in perpetuity.

VI. Both waterways are undoubtedly of supreme importance to international trade, for certain routes are shortened by thousands of miles.

VII. These artificial routes may be constituted into strategic positions of great value. There is, on the one hand, the Suez Canal, of vital importance to Great Britain as a passage through which she can maintain a safe and rapid communication with

India, Australia, and all her possessions in the East. On the other hand, the Panama Canal is in a somewhat similar position to the United States, for by means of it the voyage from her Pacific shores to those on the Atlantic, and *vice versa*, would be considerably diminished. Other powers undoubtedly have interests of this nature both at Panama and at Suez, but the matter would by no means be of such transcendent importance as it is to the United States and to Great Britain respectively.

VIII. As regards the political importance that each canal may be made to assume, they are again strikingly alike. The United States, by holding the key to the interoceanic transit, would assert thereby her moral supremacy over the Latin American Republics, thus giving bent to her policy of hegemony, which is nothing else than the amplification of the Monroe Doctrine. That Great Britain in the same manner has similar interests in Suez is undeniable.

IX. In each case foreign guarantees and protection have been sought, and, as a result, conventions have been entered into that purport to regulate the transit.

X. Finally, it may be added that in order to reconcile the various and opposing interests dependent on the question of passage, the notion of neutralisation is said to apply to these routes.

There are other points of similarity as well as of difference between the positions of the two canals. But they will be better dealt with in connection with the discussion of the treaties that establish their international status.

It is to be noticed at once, however, that the works at Panama are carried on as the national enterprise of a great state, while the Suez Canal is made and owned by a company composed of shareholders, all of whom originally were private individuals—Great Britain being now by far the largest shareholder and the only state that has a financial interest in the enterprise. But the possible bearing that this point may have on the position of an artificial waterway of this kind has already been discussed.[1]

Another point that would seem to call for notice is the fact that the international act that established the neutralisation of the Suez Canal is subscribed by the Great European Powers, the Netherlands, Spain, and Turkey; while the position of the Panama Canal is provided for by the Hay-Pauncefote treaty, entered into by Great Britain and the United States, and the Hay-Bunau-Varilla treaty, signed by the latter power and the Republic of Panama. This fact resolves itself into the question of the effectiveness or validity of neutralisation in accordance with the number of states that form part to the agreement. How far this point may affect the position of the region that is sought to be neutralised has already been dealt with.[2]

With regard to the Suez Canal, the high contracting parties "agree not to interfere" with the free use of the transit or the security of the canal, "and to respect" its plant, establishments, and buildings. It would seem, *prima facie*, that the signatory powers are not bound to oppose any

[1] See *supra*, pp. 100, 101.   [2] See *supra*, p. 89.

interference with the free use of the canal.   But, as
the principle of equality as regards the free use of
the canal formed the principal basis of the treaty,
it cannot be doubted that some one or more of the
parties to the convention would immediately come
forward if there is danger of an interruption of the
transit.   Thus it was that, even before the signing
of the convention during the Russo-Turkish War,
1877–1878, the British Government seized the
occasion to make it known that any attempt to
interfere with the canal or its approaches would be
regarded "as a menace to India and a grave injury
to the commerce of the world," and further, that
"Her Majesty's Government are firmly determined not to permit the canal to be made the
scene of any combat or warlike operations."
Whereupon Russia declared that "the imperial
cabinet will neither blockade nor interrupt, nor
in any way menace, the navigation of the Suez
Canal."[1]

In the Panama Canal Convention it is provided
that the "United States adopts" certain rules as
the basis of neutralisation. The effect of this
phraseology, however, has already been discussed.[2]

It would be profitable now to compare the
provisions of the two treaties so as to observe at
once their similarities and differences, and thus, after
placing side by side the rules, to add a few
explanations that may seem to suggest themselves.

[1] Quoted by Hains, *op. cit.* and *loc. cit.* p. 386.
[2] See *supra*, p. 113.

HAY-PAUNCEFOTE CONVENTION.	CONSTANTINOPLE CONVENTION.
"The canal shall be free and open to the vessels of commerce and of war of all nations observing these rules on terms of entire equality, so that there shall be no discrimination against any such nation, or its citizens or subjects, in respect of the conditions or charges of traffic or otherwise. Such conditions and charges of traffic shall be just and equitable."	"The Suez maritime Canal shall always be free and open in time of war as in time of peace, to every vessel of commerce or of war, without distinction of flag. Consequently, the high contracting parties agree not in any way to interfere with the free use of the canal, in time of war as in time of peace."

As has already been pointed out, in the Convention of Constantinople there occur the words "in time of war as in time of peace," with reference to the freedom of the canal. It has been too hastily argued by some that no provision is to be found in the Hay-Pauncefote treaty so as to lay it down that the Panama Canal should be open in case of a war to which the United States is a party. To those who hold this view, it must be answered that it is evident that many of the rules of the Hay-Pauncefote treaty can only come into force by a state of war, and that therefore they are made to be applied to belligerents. Besides, in Rule 6 of the Hay-Pauncefote Convention, it is enacted that "the plant, establishments, buildings, and all work necessary to the construction, maintenance, and operation of the canal . . . *in time of war as in time of peace*, shall enjoy complete immunity from attack or injury by belligerents, and from acts calculated to impair their usefulness as part of the canal."[1] Is it possible, in the face of this provision, to think that the canal can be closed to belligerents when they conform to the rules of the treaty?

[1] Article III., Rule 6.

" The canal shall never be blockaded, nor shall any right of war be
exercised nor any act of hostility
be committed within it.   The
United States, however, shall be
at liberty to maintain such military
police along the canal as may be
necessary to protect it against lawlessness and disorder."

" The canal shall never be subjected to the exercise of the right
of blockade.   The maritime canal
remaining open in time of war, as
a free passage, even to the ships
of war of belligerents . . . the
high contracting parties agree that
no right of war, no act of hostility,
nor any act having for its object
to obstruct the free navigation of
the canal, shall be committed in
the canal or its ports of access, as
well as within a radius of three
marine miles from those ports,
even though the Ottoman Empire
should be one of the belligerent
powers."

It is not difficult to meet the suggestion that the
canal may be closed to an enemy of the United States,
because there are no specific terms in the Hay-
Pauncefote treaty enjoining that the rules of freedom
of transit and the absence of hostile acts in the canal
should also apply to this particular case.   In the expression of ideas two courses are possible when it is
sought to make an absolute statement of universal
application.   One of such courses is to make the
assertion in general terms (thereby including all the
possible objects to which the statement refers), and
then proceed by a sort of emphatic redundance to
lay it down that the general assertion applies to the
same extent to an object which is already included,
and had some particular relation to the question
about which the statement is made.   This is the case
of the provision in the Convention of Constantinople,
for it reads as follows : " The high contracting
parties agree that no right of war, no act of hostility,
nor any act having for its object to obstruct the free

navigation of the canal, shall be committed . . .
even though the *Ottoman Empire* should be one of
the belligerents."[1]

It is submitted, therefore, that the Government
of the Porte, being one of the contracting parties, the
addition of the phrase "even though the Ottoman
Empire should be one of the belligerents" is re-
dundant, and hence was not strictly necessary in
order to ascertain the meaning of the provision.   On
the other hand, the other possible course to which
reference has been made, is to make the statement in
general terms, including all the objects, as in the
previous case, and then state the only exceptions, if
any, or the sole deviations that are permitted, in a
manner that would leave no doubt that a certain
object that stands in a special position as regards
the matter in hand is also bound by the general
provision.   This was the course adopted by the
signatories of the Hay-Pauncefote treaty.   They laid
it down that "the canal shall never be blockaded,
nor shall any right of war be exercised nor any act
of hostility be committed within it.   The United
States, *however*,[2] shall be at liberty to maintain such
military police along the canal as may be necessary
to protect it against lawlessness and disorder."   The
United States was one of the contracting parties, and
she has also a special relation to the Panama Canal,
owing to the fact that she is carrying on the works.
The first statement here quoted clearly includes the
United States, and the second one lays down the
only relaxation—which, by the way, is very restricted
—that exists from the general principle ; this restricted

[1] Article IV.   [2] Italics are the author's.

exception goes to show in a clear manner, by implication, that no act of hostility is to be committed within the canal even by the United States in the event of war to which they are parties.

Perhaps some persons would be wondering by now how it is that the United States have gone to the enormous expense of this undertaking if they cannot profit by it in the event of a war, so as to crush their enemies who attempted to pass the waters of the canal. This point is not relevant to our inquiry. From the purely *legal* standpoint, it must be stated in an unequivocal manner that in theory the belligerent vessels of a potential enemy of the United States are entitled to cross the canal unmolested. Between theory and fact, of course, there is sometimes a great chasm. From the point of view of fact, it would be impossible for a nation at war with the United States to send its belligerent vessels through the canal. It must be remembered that the United States have the exclusive right of providing for the management of the canal; the persons engaged in the operations would be, therefore, officials of that power. Now it is obvious that since the canal is to be open only to those nations who observe the rules of the convention, it follows that they cannot demand the removal of those officials. And what power at war with the United States would send its belligerent vessels across the canal knowing that they are going to encounter at every step a *possible enemy*? Such persons engaged in the operation and management of the canal may not be combatants,—under no circumstances could they be *lawful* combatants—but this fact will not alter a possibility of danger that no nation would lose sight of. The obvious inference is, of course, that the canal shall not be used by a belligerent who is an enemy of the United States. This peculiar position of the United States in respect of the Panama Canal from the point of view of fact, finds a close parallelism in the advantageous situation that Great Britain holds in relation to the Suez Canal. In theory, all British enemies are entitled to pass through Suez. But matters are different in practice, for it would mean utter ruin to the belligerent vessels of a nation at war with Great Britain if they attempted to use the canal whilst the latter power holds impregnable positions at the approaches of the route. Gibraltar, Malta, and Bab-el-Mandeb are to the British cause what the locks in Panama would be to the United States.

"Vessels of war of a belligerent shall not revictual nor take any stores in the canal except so far as may be strictly necessary, and the transit of such vessels through the canal shall be affected with the least possible delay, in accordance with the regulations in force, and with only such intermission as may result from the necessities of the service. Prizes shall be in all respects subject to the same rules as vessels of war of the belligerents."

"No belligerent shall embark or disembark troops, or munitions of war, or warlike materials in the canal, except in case of accidental hindrance of the transit, and in

"Vessels of war of belligerents shall not revictual or take in stores in the canal and its ports of access, except in so far as may be strictly necessary. The transit of the aforesaid vessels through the canal shall be effected with the least possible delay, in accordance with the regulations in force, and without any other intermission than that resulting from the necessities of the service."

"Prizes shall be subjected in all respects to the same rules as the vessels of war of belligerents."

"In time of war belligerent powers shall not disembark nor embark within the canal and its ports of access, either troops, munitions, or materials of war.

such case the transit shall be resumed with all possible dispatch."

All these provisions " shall apply to waters adjacent to the canal, within three marine miles of either end. Vessels of war of a belligerent shall not remain in such waters longer than twenty-four hours at any one time except in case of distress, and, in such case, shall depart as soon as possible ; but a vessel of war of one belligerent shall not depart within twenty-four hours from the departure of a vessel of war of the other belligerent."

" The plant, establishments, buildings, and all work necessary to the construction, maintenance, and operation of the canal shall be deemed to be part thereof, for the purpose of this treaty, and in time of war, as in time of peace, shall enjoy complete immunity from attack or injury by belligerents, and from acts calculated to impair their usefulness as part of the canal."

(The Hay-Pauncefote treaty is silent on this point.)

But in case of an accidental hindrance in the canal, men may be embarked or disembarked at the ports of access by detachments not exceeding 1000 men, with a corresponding amount of war material."

" The stay of vessels of war of belligerents at Port Said and in the roadstead of Suez shall not exceed twenty-four hours, except in case of distress. In such case they shall be bound to leave as soon as possible. An interval of twenty-four hours shall always elapse between the sailing of a belligerent ship from one of the ports of access and the departure of a ship belonging to the hostile power."

" The high contracting parties likewise undertake to respect the plant, establishments, buildings, and works of the Maritime Canal and of the Freshwater Canal."

" The powers shall not keep any vessels of war in the waters of the canal. Nevertheless, they may station vessels of war in the ports of access of Port Said and Suez, the number of which shall not exceed two for each power. This right shall not be exercised by belligerents."[1]

---

[1] This provision can hardly be said to be essential to neutralisation. Besides, the right to station vessels of war is partly admitted by the provision itself.

(The Hay-Pauncefote treaty is silent on this point.)

"The high contracting parties undertake to bring the present treaty to the knowledge of the states which have not signed it, inviting them to accede to it." [1]

There are still other provisions in the Convention of Constantinople, but they are practically of no interest in this connection. They deal with the measures that Turkey and Egypt might take in case it should become necessary to defend the canal or the Ottoman possessions situated in the eastern coast of the Red Sea. They will be dealt with in the next chapter.

After noticing the numerous and important characteristics of the analogy existing between the Suez and Panama Canals, it seems impossible to avoid the conclusion that their position in law will be exactly the same.

[1] It should be noticed at once that an article similar to this had been included in the original treaty signed by Mr. Hay and Lord Pauncefote, February 5, 1900, but it was struck out by the Senate. In the treaty entered into by the same plenipotentiaries in the following year, the article did not appear (cp. Moore, *Digest of International Law*, vol. iii. pp. 210 and 211). Much significance should not be attached to the omission of any such provision, for it must be kept in mind that the United States have persistently objected to allowing European powers to meddle in American affairs. They permitted England to do so, but they were forced by the special circumstances which have been noticed in the course of this essay.

CHAPTER VI.

THE FORTIFICATION OF THE PANAMA CANAL.[1]

THE status of neutralisation, as has been seen, carries with it certain consequences, some of which are well defined by International Law. These are dependent for their existence, like the principal notion itself, upon treaty stipulations, and therefore no doubt should exist with regard to them, if the conventional agreements are clear and devoid of ambiguities. But there may be also some other conceptions that are deemed, rightly or wrongly, to be the necessary effects of the theory of neutralisation, about which no certainty can exist, owing to the fact that this branch of law is comparatively modern and has not yet been fully developed; or because the international documents from which they derive their force are silent upon the subject, or not sufficiently precise and free from obscurity. When this is the case such notions belong to the arena of debate, and the duty of the international jurist should be to state both sides of the controversy, and attempt the solution of the difficulty from general principles, taking into

[1] See, e.g., George W. Davies, "Fortifications at Panama," in the *American Journal of International Law*, vol. iii. pp. 885 et seq.; H. S. Knapp, "The Real Status of the Panama Canal as regards Neutralisation," in *The American Journal of International Law*, vol. iv. pp. 314 et. seq.

consideration ᵥthe tendencies of the development of the law. The question as to whether a neutralised region may or may not be fortified remains yet in the field of speculation. It is intended in this chapter to deal with the subject in a general manner, and then discuss it more specifically in connection with the Panama Canal. Owing to the special circumstances of the case, which have already been noted, the answer to our inquiry is necessarily obscure and cannot be laid down with dogmatic precision.

The question as to how far, or to what extent, if at all, the notion of neutralisation would be affected by the fact that the thing neutralised is fortified, would seem to resolve itself into the following : Is the erection of fortifications repugnant to the non-belligerent idea that forms the essential characteristic of neutralisation? Or, in other words, how do the general principles of the law, the practice of nations, or the opinion of writers deal with this question?

The notion of neutralisation, as has been pointed out, has been made to serve various ends. There is one point, however, that is common to all. It is the freedom from the belligerent character that they may normally have. Thus the state, person, or thing neutralised is entitled to enjoy the benefit of peace, but, on the other hand, is burdened with the corresponding obligation of not taking part in a war. It is clear that the non-belligerent idea is the essential characteristic of the notion. But, obviously enough, the right of self-defence is reserved ; this is a primordial right that the province of law cannot suppress or suspend. Law cannot discourage self-help, for then the law-abiding members of the community would be at the entire mercy of wrong-doers.

Neutralisation, then, cannot take away the right of self-defence. It is well known that Belgium and Switzerland are permanently neutralised, and that nevertheless they are ready to defend their integrity by well - organised armies. The fact that both these countries keep a regular organisation for defence can in no way affect their international status. And this is quite in line with the modern tendencies and aspirations of law. Advanced constitutions expressly lay it down that every citizen is entitled to carry arms. A man may be armed for defensive purposes, and there is no basis for the presumption that he is going to commit a breach of the peace. The right to carry arms, of course, does not mean that a person may attack another—it is simply the right of self-defence sanctioned by the fundamental laws. In the same way the presence of regular armies in Belgium and Switzerland should not be taken to mean that they are to be made use of for offensive purposes. Undoubtedly arms may be instruments of attack or of protection, but the former alternative ought not to be the first to be taken into consideration when there is an international agreement that forbids offensive measures.

Now, passing from the question of the presence of armies in a neutralised region to that of fortifications, one would feel bound to assert that the analogy is real, and that the logical consequences that can be drawn from it are well based, and, therefore, convincing. Belligerent organisations such as armies are, indeed, more likely to be used for offensive purposes than fortifications, for the simple reason that the former are capable of movement while the latter are fixed, and therefore cannot come into action unless they happen to be in the scene of battle. International Law allows the existence of war implements and armies in neutralised regions. *Prima facie* the presence of military elements in a place would seem to be incompatible with its non-belligerent character, but a little consideration on the conception of self-defence necessarily shows that no contradiction or inconsistency occurs. We have seen that private law recognises the right of self-help, even though private warfare is prohibited, and, in case of wrong-doing, this law has the power and the means of inflicting the corresponding punishment. In the case of International Law the reasons that may be brought forward against the curtailment of this right are still stronger. Here war is allowed and regulated by the law itself. It is true that among the civilised communities the rule of *bellum omnium contra omnes* does not hold good, but still the law of nations has not yet reached the same stage of development as private law, and therefore the doctrine of self-redress would be, and in fact is, more prominent in the former than in the latter.

It would be interesting to deal with other cases of neutralisation in order to see whether the precedents established by the position of Belgium and Switzerland have been followed.

In the Treaty of Paris for the neutralisation of the Black Sea it is said that "the maintenance or establishment upon its coast of military-maritime arsenals become alike unnecessary and purposeless," and hence

Russia and Turkey engaged themselves not to establish or maintain armaments upon it.[1] But, as has already been pointed out, this case cannot be taken as a precedent, because the so-called ostensible neutrality of the Black Sea was not a real neutralisation, but simply a veiled restriction on the sovereignty of Russia for no general purpose whatever.

By the treaty neutralising the Ionian Islands, 1863, it is provided that "the fortifications constructed in the Island of Corfu and its immediate dependencies being purposeless henceforth, shall be demolished."[2] It is to be noticed, however, that in the treaty signed by the powers and Greece in the following year no reference is made to fortifications; the King of Greece only promised "to maintain such neutrality." It is indeed a nice question to decide whether these islands are neutralised. Greece draws men and supplies from them; and the opinion has been advanced that a power at war with her would be free to attack and occupy them.[3]

Argentine and Chile, in their treaty of 1881 that purports to neutralise the Straits of Magellan, have caused a clause to be introduced whereby, in order to "ensure this liberty (of navigation) and neutrality, no fortifications or military defences shall be erected that could interfere with this object."[4] We have already given our reasons for asserting that the Straits of Magellan are not endowed with the privileges of neutralisation.

Based perhaps on the consideration of the above

[1] Article 13.   [2] Article 3.
[3] See Lawrence, *The Principles of International Law*, 4th edition, p. 603.
[4] Article 5.

cases, some writers have used language that would leave no doubt as to the illegality of erecting fortifications in a neutral region. Thus Professor Moore asserts that "the idea of neutrality or of neutralisation has usually been deemed incompatible even with the mere maintenance of armed forces and fortifications." But he limits considerably the meaning of his statements—or perhaps even destroys them—by saying that the erection of "fortifications, even if no offensive or hostile use of them be intended for the purpose of preserving neutrality, is novel in public law."[1] The notion of neutralisation is novel, and, in the words of Professor Oppenheim, "it remains to be seen whether it can stand the test of history."[2] We need not be surprised, therefore, if the idea of erecting fortifications or of maintaining armed forces in a neutralised place is of modern growth. In any case there cannot be any doubt, for all writers have agreed upon it, that the neutralisation of Belgium and Switzerland is an accepted fact that has passed to the domain of International Law, in spite of the existence in both countries of standing armies.

Professor Latané, dealing with the different characteristics of neutralisation, says that it "implies the absence of fortifications." And he states further that "the mere existence of fortifications would impeach the good faith of the parties to the agreement."[3] Mr. Hains holds undoubtedly the same view, for in his examination of the status of the Panama Canal he submits that, "according to the generally accepted opinions, there can be no neutral-

---

[1] Quoted by Hains, *op. cit.* and *loc. cit.* pp. 368–369.
[2] *International Law*, vol. i. p. 144.   [3] *Op. cit.* and *loc. cit.*

isation with fortifications, and, *vice versa*, the erection of fortifications destroys neutralisation."[1] As a matter of criticism it can well be suggested that Professor Latané's assertion is open to doubt. It seems too absolute to arrive at such a conclusion, since others are also possible which, in truth, are more in accordance with the facts; for, if a nation has given its formal promise not to use a certain place for hostile purposes, more definite manifestations that the erection of fortifications—which may, without any great effort of the mind, be constructed for the preservation of the neutrality which the treaty ensures—should be forthcoming before such a serious accusation is formulated.

By the time of the conclusion of the Convention of Constantinople, 1888, a more reasonable view of the question of defence in the case of a violation of neutrality had been evolved. For in that treaty it was provided that the ordinary rules forbidding the commission of acts of hostility, the exercise of any right of war, or the stationing of war vessels in the canal, or its approaches, were to be of no effect if it should become necessary for the Sultan or the Khedive to take measures for ensuring the protection and free use of the canal, or for the "defence of Egypt and the maintenance of public order," as well as the defence of the Sultan's possessions situated on the eastern coast of the Red Sea. But there is a proviso to the effect that these measures should never be allowed to interfere with the freedom of transit. The treaty, it is true, specially forbids the erection of permanent fortifications. But the right of self-

---

[1] *Op. cit.* and *loc. cit.* p. 384.

defence is expressly excepted. It must be remembered that elaborate provisions are formulated
in order to recognise the power of disregarding the
strict neutrality of the route, when the safety of the
transit is threatened.

The question of the fortification of the Panama
Canal is not mentioned in the Hay-Pauncefote treaty
of 1901. In the Clayton-Bulwer Convention a clause
is found that prevents the fortification of the waterway. And in the first draft of the Hay-Pauncefote
treaty of February 5, 1900, the same provision
occurs, and, besides, a declaration that is intended
to make the rules of neutrality not applicable "to
measures which the United States may find it
necessary to take for securing by its own forces the
defence of the United States and the maintenance of
public order." This declaratory provision, which had
been inserted by the Senate of the United States,
was objected to by His Majesty's Government
because, in the words of Lord Lansdowne, then
Foreign Secretary, it would "involve a distinct
departure from the principles of neutralisation."[1]   In
consequence of this the United States no longer
pressed for the inclusion of the clause, and hence it
does not appear in the finally accepted treaty.[2]   Lord
Lansdowne had also pointed out the ambiguity that
would result if one clause permitted the adoption of

---

[1] Memorandum of Lord Lansdowne to Mr. Lowther, August 3,
1901, *Parl. Pap., United States*, No. 1, 1902, 2.

[2] It may be remarked here that Great Britain's conduct in this
connection is very suggestive. It plainly shows that His Majesty's
Government entered into the engagement with the understanding that
the United States would not use the canal for the purpose of *national*
defence.

defensive measures, while another prohibited the erection of fortifications. Finally, the provision that prevented the fortification of the canal as contained in the Hay-Pauncefote treaty of February 5, 1900, does not appear in the draft that was ultimately accepted by the two governments. The only provision that has reference to the defence of the canal is one that has already been noticed, and runs as follows: "The United States, however, shall be at liberty to maintain such military police along the canal as may be necessary to protect it against lawlessness and disorder."

It becomes evident from this provision, as well as from the clear intention of the contracting parties at the time of the negotiation, that the United States are not permitted to exercise in the canal any right of war or commit any act of hostility against a possible enemy, when such action would have only in view the defence of the United States. In fact the treaty does not expressly authorise the United States to commit any hostile action even with the purpose of protecting the route. But by implication, since they can maintain there a body of "military police" to prevent "lawlessness and disorder," the United States would seem to be empowered to go to any extent of violence, if the circumstances should so require, in order to defend the waterway.

It must be confessed that the treaty is lacking in rules explanatory of the measures that should be taken in case it should become necessary to protect the canal. It may be thought, perhaps, that any such rules are not required, owing to the existence of accepted principles of law that sanction any conduct that is reasonable and strictly directed to self-defence. Lord Lansdowne well perceived the absence of provisions of this nature, and perhaps for this reason he commented on the circumstances in the following manner :—

"I understand that by the omission of all reference to the matter of defence, the United States Government desire to reserve the power of taking measures to protect the canal, at any time when the United States may be at war, from destruction or damage at the hands of an enemy or enemies. On the other hand, I conclude that, with the above exception, there is no intention to derogate from the principles of neutrality laid down by the rules. As to the first of these propositions, I am not prepared to deny that contingencies may arise when not only from a national point of view, but on behalf of the commercial interests of the whole world, it might be of supreme importance to the United States that they should be free to adopt measures for the defence of the canal at a moment when they were themselves engaged in hostilities." [1]

This explanation, if such it can be called, is derived from the pen of a diplomatist, and hence it does not concede a great deal. The possibility of an event that may call for the protection or defence of the canal is thereby recognised ; but as to the measures that should then be adopted nothing is said. The explanation, therefore, is as vague as words can make it. From another point of view, however, Lord Lansdowne's note cannot be taken to imply that the United States would be free to adopt *any measures* that can be directed to the protection of the canal. No right to fortify the canal or its approaches is expressly granted by the treaty, nor can such a right be made out from the statement just quoted.

[1] Memorandum of Lord Lansdowne to Mr. Lowther, *op. cit.*

In the treaty concluded between the Republic of Panama and the United States of America, more mention is made with regard to the protection of the canal than in the Hay-Pauncefote Convention. One of the articles of this treaty runs as follows :—

"*If it should become necessary*[1] at any time to employ armed forces for the safety or protection of the canal, or of the ships that make use of the same, or the railways and auxiliary works, the United States shall have the right, at all times and in its discretion, to use its police and its land and naval forces, or to establish fortifications for these purposes."[2]

It is evident from the above provision that the contracting parties decided to make the article conditional. That is to say, the United States are empowered to commit acts of hostility, and even to establish fortifications, "if it should become necessary . . . for the safety or protection of the canal." The treaty does not thereby grant the right to erect permanent fortifications, but it may be a question whether fortifications that are not permanent would be adequate for the purpose of defence at the present time. It is not difficult to foresee that the United States are inclined to take all needful precautions so as to avoid a surprise that would mean an enormous loss of capital to them and a considerable inconvenience to every trading nation of the globe. It is only natural that they should do so. But this is a question that is hardly relevant to our purpose. Neither is it intended to discuss here whether the United States would be entitled to set up in their works a moderate number of medium calibre guns or, instead, "monumental" forts armed with the most

---

[1] The italics are the author's.   [2] Article xxiii.

powerful guns of the day.[1] Suffice it to say, therefore, that the United States are backed by a conventional agreement with the Republic of Panama
for the purpose of taking the measures that would be
required in order to defend effectively the trans-
isthmian canal.

It further appears that this clause relative to the
possible fortification of the Panama Canal is not in
opposition to the provisions of the Hay-Pauncefote
treaty. This treaty, it is true, is silent on the
question of fortifications as well as on the employment of "armed forces," and, therefore, it seems that
the United States are left free to take reasonable
measures for the defence of the waterway, for, it
must be borne in mind, the right of self-defence
cannot be taken away either by treaty or by implica-
tions resulting from the interpretation of other
principles of International Law.

It has been suggested in some quarters[2] that it is
better for the United States not to fortify the canal,
because, according to a provision of the Hague Convention, 1909, "the bombardment by naval forces
of undefended ports, towns, villages, dwellings, or
buildings, is forbidden." The canal would be free
from attack, it is argued, if it is not fortified; whereas
the fact of its fortification would open the way for
its possible bombardment by a belligerent. It must
be remembered, however, that the object pursued in
neutralising a waterway is not only to prevent that it

[1] Cp. Admiral Sir Cyprian Bridge, "Naval Strategy and the
Panama Canal," article in *The Times*, South American Supplement,
Nov. 29, 1910.
[2] Hains, *op. cit.* and *loc. cit.* p. 389.

should be attacked. The primordial object, as has been often pointed out, is to secure freedom of transit. It is evident that in spite of the waterway being *legally* free from attack (as would be the case if it is not fortified) it is yet possible for a state at war with another to act in a manner so as to prevent that the canal should be freely used by all vessels at all times. For if a recalcitrant state should decide to disregard the neutrality of the canal, it could proceed to blockade it, direct that its vessels should revictual or take stores therein, or embark and disembark troops or munitions of war, without in any way infringing the provision of the Hague Convention to which reference has been made. The absence of fortifications at Panama, therefore, would not by itself secure the purpose for which the canal is endowed with the privileges and liabilities of neutralisation.[1]

The question as to whether the Panama Canal should be fortified or not is a matter of policy that concerns the states interested. The inquiry here attempted is merely directed to discover whether the

[1] It may be interesting to call the attention of the reader to a provision to be found in the Declaration concerning Egypt and Morocco entered into by Great Britain and France, of April 8, 1904. The article in question reads as follows : "A fin d'assurer le libre passage au détroit de Gibraltar, les deux gouvernements conviennent de ne pas laisser élever des fortifications ou des ouvrages strategiques quelconques sur la côte marocaine comprise entre Melilla et les hauteurs qui dominent la rive droite du Sebou exclusivement" ("Les Accords Franco-Anglais du Avril 8, 1904," *Appreciation critique*, Paris, 1905). It is not difficult to see that this provision is nothing else than a diplomatic euphemism. The ostensible purpose for restricting the erection of fortifications is said to be "in order to ensure free passage by the Strait of Gibraltar." Evidently free passage there is not guaranteed ; nor did the contracting powers intend in any way to secure that free transit of which the provision speaks.

fortification of the Panama Canal would affect its neutralisation. And in this respect it may be laid down that if the arguments adduced are in any way correct, the answer would necessarily be in the negative. Neutralisation, or in fact any other conception of International Law, cannot take away the right of self-defence, and, as a logical consequence, the erection of fortifications is not repugnant to the notion of neutralisation.

CHAPTER VII.

CONCLUSION.

It may be needful in an inquiry of this nature to trace in a single chapter the successive steps that have been traversed, so as to consider as a whole the entire structure, which may appear in its detached parts somewhat confused on account of its various details.

A recapitulation of the previous chapters reducing to concise statements the results of our inquiry would not only help us to attain precision and coherence, but also assist in showing the connection that exists between the different parts. On more than one occasion, however, when dealing with the application of certain principles or the interpretation of international treaties, diplomatic dispatches, or historical facts, the conclusions that seemed to follow logically from them have been immediately recorded. Nevertheless, it is deemed advisable to add an organised re-statement of the general conclusions that the premises separately adduced seem to warrant, but avoiding, as far as possible, the repetition of the arguments themselves. The scope of this chapter is, therefore, to present the whole logical fabric so as to contemplate it from a distance.

The policy of the United States towards the canal question has passed gradually but progressively from indifference to intense interest. Vital considerations connected with their extraordinary development have induced them, especially towards the later part of their career, to attempt to apply to the subject of interoceanic communication the flexible principles of their foreign policy which are supposed to rest on President Monroe's Message. It seemed for a moment that they were bent on acquiring an *exclusive* control of the canal, so that it should he managed and regulated as an integral part of their territory. But the general interests that other nations have in the question of transit, together with the return to a spirit of fairness, have finally led the North American Republic to recognise the tendencies of some modern rules of International Law that grant to all nations at all times the right of passage by what are considered to be the world's thoroughfares.

The whole history of the endeavours of certain powers to appropriate to themselves the exclusive benefit of using the maritime communication is sufficient in itself to demonstrate fully that the artificial route should be included in the domain of that law that regulates the intercourse of the general body of civilised nations. Indeed, no other course is possible in order to reconcile the conflicting interests that would necessarily spring from such a problem.

The question could not be dealt with by the territorial power alone on account of the special circumstances of the case, nor could it be assimilated to natural straits so as to make the general rules adopted for them applicable to it. The problem, it has been shown, is *sui generis* in its very nature, and special rules for the regulation of the transit had to be evolved.

The notion of neutralisation, therefore, has been thought to apply to such a case. But this conception as applied to states or parts of states is found to be different from the one that should be applied to a region where freedom of transit is to be attained. In consequence of this fact the essential characteristics of the notion—freedom from hostilities—has been retained, and special conventional provisions have been added so as to insure the general purposes of the law.

In order to establish neutralisation, it is necessary that there should exist a general interest among the different nations of the globe with regard to a certain region. This interest has undoubtedly been shown to exist towards the Panama Canal. On account of this interest and because the Hay-Pauncefote treaty, although entered into by Great Britain and the United States only, embodies rules which have already gained universal acceptance and are just in themselves, it is submitted that the provisions contained in it have come to be of a law-making force. This international agreement is supported by the tacit understanding of all the other members of the family of nations—a fact that makes it binding on all states. Professor Westlake comments on this subject in the following manner: " To the system thus established for the Central American Canal of the future the express assent of the European States has not been invited. Their assent may be assumed from their own establishment of the same system in the old

world, and because the concurrence of the two great
powers of North America must carry for that part of
the new world something of the same authority which
the concurrence of the great powers carries for the
old, especially with relation to a waterway so vitally
affecting the communication between the Atlantic
and the Pacific coasts of each. We may treat the
conditions, under which interoceanic canals can be
made conducive to commerce and all peaceful development, as being henceforth an ascertained part
of International Law."[1]

It has also been seen that the treaties in existence
dealing with the position of the Panama Canal are
entered into by the states more directly concerned,
and contain the essential features of neutralisation.

One of such treaties (the Hay-Pauncefote) was
framed avowedly taking the Convention of Constantinople as its model. It is hardly necessary to
insist on the fact that there is a real analogy between
the Panama and Suez Canals. And since the Suez
Canal is undoubtedly a neutralised waterway, it
necessarily follows that this legal status would be
applied *mutatis mutandis* to the Panama Canal. It
will be interesting to quote here the words of Doctor
Lawrence, who argues that since Great Britain and
the United States have embodied in the Hay-Pauncefote treaty " provisions already accepted with regard
to the Suez Canal by the civilised world, it is exceedingly improbable that objections will be raised against
the same provisions when applied to the only other
canal of the like kind on the face of the earth."[2]

[1] *International Law*, Part I, pp. 330, 331.
[2] *The Principles of International Law*, 4th ed. 1910, p. 201.

The opinion has further been advanced that the non-belligerent idea that forms the essential characteristic of the notion of neutralisation cannot imply the suspension of the right of self-defence, and as a corollary of this, the erection of fortifications, should the Panama Canal ever be fortified, cannot be said to be incompatible with its neutralisation.

It is not possible, in the face of such evidence as that here adduced, to avoid the conclusion that the Panama Canal is endowed with the privileges and liabilities of neutralisation. Professor Oppenheim has already put it in terse and forcible language. The Hay-Pauncefote treaty of 1901, he says, "neutralises permanently the Panama Canal of the future."[1] The freedom of navigation for all vessels of all nations, and at all times, by what are considered to be the highways of the world, is a principle deeply entwined in the roots of International Law. It cannot be otherwise, for on it depends that natural intercourse among nations which is of such vital importance for the maintenance of those relations which International Law attempts to regulate. Therefore, even quite apart from the weighty moral considerations that may be adduced in favour of neutralisation as restricting the area of hostilities, and thus extending, although in a small degree, the blessing of peace, it may be said that on general legal grounds, as has been remarked by a learned authority, the "great majority of writers on the subject are strong advocates of neutralisation, and this principle is certainly in line with the tendencies of International Law."[2]

---

[1] *International Law*, vol. i. p. 568.   [2] Latané, *op. cit.* and *loc. cit.*

APPENDICES

APPENDIX I.

TREATY OF PEACE, AMITY, NAVIGATION, AND COM-
MERCE, BETWEEN THE UNITED STATES AND
NEW GRANADA, ESTABLISHING THE NEUTRAL-
ISATION OF THE ISTHMUS OF PANAMA.

Concluded December 12, 1846.

ARTICLE XXXV.

THE United States of America and the Republic of New
Granada, desiring to make as durable as possible the relations
which are to be established between the two parties by virtue
of this treaty, have declared solemnly and do agree to the
following points:—

1st. For the better understanding of the preceding
articles, it is and has been stipulated between the high contracting parties that the citizens, vessels, and merchandise of
the United States shall enjoy in the ports of New Granada,
including those of the part of the Granadian territory
generally denominated *Isthmus of Panama*, from its southern-
most extremity until the boundary of Costa Rica, all the
exemptions, privileges, and immunities concerning commerce
and navigation which are now or may hereafter be enjoyed
by Granadian citizens, their vessels or merchandise; and
that this equality of favours shall be made to extend to the
passengers, correspondence, and merchandise of the United
States in their transit across the said territory from one sea
to the other. The government of New Granada guarantees
to the government of the United States that the right of way
or transit across the Isthmus of Panama, upon any modes of
communication that now exist or that may hereafter be
constructed, shall be open and free to the government and
citizens of the United States, and for the transportation of

any articles of produce, manufactures, or merchandise, of lawful commerce, belonging to the citizens of the United States: that no other tolls or charges shall be levied or collected upon the citizens of the United States, or their said merchandise thus passing over any road or canal that may be made by the government of New Granada, or by the authority of the same, than is, under like circumstances, levied upon or collected from the Granadian citizens; that any lawful produce, manufactures, or merchandise belonging to citizens of the United States thus passing from one sea to the other, in either direction, for the purpose of exportation to any other foreign country, shall not be liable to any import duties whatever; or, having paid such duties, they shall be entitled to drawback upon their exportation; nor shall the citizens of the United States be liable to any duties, tolls, or charges of any kind to which native citizens are not subjected for thus passing the said isthmus. And, in order to secure to themselves the tranquil and constant enjoyment of these advantages, and as an especial compensation for the said advantages, and for the favours they have acquired by the 4th, 5th, and 6th Articles of this treaty, the United States guarantee positively and efficaciously to New Granada, by the present stipulation, the perfect neutrality of the before-mentioned isthmus, with the view that the free transit from the one to the other sea may not be interrupted or embarrassed in any future time while this treaty exists; and, in consequence, the United States also guarantee, in the same manner, the rights of sovereignty and property which New Granada has and possesses over the said territory.

              B. A. BIDLACK.   (Seal)
              M. M. MALLARINO. (Seal)

APPENDIX II.

CONVENTION BETWEEN THE UNITED STATES AND
GREAT BRITAIN FOR FACILITATING AND PRO-
TECTING THE CONSTRUCTION OF A SHIP CANAL
BETWEEN THE ATLANTIC AND THE PACIFIC
OCEANS AND FOR OTHER PURPOSES (CLAYTON-
BULWER).

Concluded April 19, 1850.

THE United States and Her Britannic Majesty, being
desirous of consolidating the relations of amity which so
happily subsist between them, by setting forth and fixing in
a convention their views and intentions with reference to any
means of communication by ship canal which may be constructed between the Atlantic and the Pacific Oceans, by the
way of the river San Juan de Nicaragua, and either or both
of the Lakes of Nicaragua or Managua, to any port or place
in the Pacific Ocean ; the President of the United States
has conferred full powers on John M. Clayton, Secretary
of States of the United States, and Her Britannic Majesty
on the Right Honourable Sir Henry Lytton Bulwer, a
member of Her Majesty's Most Honourable Privy Council,
Knight Commander of the Most Honourable Order of the
Bath, and Envoy Extraordinary and Minister Plenipotentiary of Her Britannic Majesty to the United States, for
the aforesaid purpose ; and the said plenipotentiaries having
exchanged their full powers, which were found to be in
proper form, have agreed to the following articles :—

ARTICLE I.

The governments of the United States and Great Britain
hereby declare that neither the one nor the other will ever

obtain or maintain for itself any exclusive control over the said ship canal, agreeing that neither will ever erect or maintain any fortifications commanding the same or in the vicinity thereof, or occupy, or fortify, or colonise, or assume, or exercise any dominion over Nicaragua, Costa Rica, the Mosquito Coast, or any part of Central America; nor will either make use of any protection which either affords or may afford, or any alliance which either has or may have to or with any state or people, for the purpose of erecting or maintaining any such fortifications, or of occupying, fortifying, or colonising Nicaragua, Costa Rica, the Mosquito Coast, or any part of Central America, or of assuming or exercising dominion over the same; nor will the United States or Great Britain take advantage of any intimacy, or use any alliance, connection, or influence that either may possess with any state or government through whose territory the said canal may pass, for the purpose of acquiring or holding, directly or indirectly, for the citizens or subjects of the one, any rights or advantages in regard to commerce or navigation through the said canal which shall not be offered on the same terms to the citizens or subjects of the other.

Article II.

Vessels of the United States or Great Britain, traversing the said canal, shall, in case of war between the contracting parties, be exempted from blockade, detention, or capture, by either of the belligerents; and this provision shall extend to such a distance from the two ends of the said canal, as may hereafter be found expedient to establish.

Article III.

In order to secure the construction of the said canal, the contracting parties engage that, if any such canal shall be undertaken upon fair and equitable terms by any parties having the authority of the local government or governments, through whose territory the same may pass, then the persons employed in making the said canal, and their property used, for that object, shall be protected, from the commencement of the said canal to its completion, by the government of the United States and Great Britain, from unjust detention, confiscation, seizure, or any violence whatsoever.

ARTICLE IV.

The contracting parties will use whatever influence they respectively exercise, with any state, states, or governments possessing or claiming to possess any jurisdiction or right over the territory which the said canal will traverse, or which shall be near the waters applicable thereto, in order to induce such states or governments to facilitate the construction of the said canal by every means in their power. And furthermore, the United States and Great Britain agree to use their good offices, wherever or however it may be most expedient, in order to procure the establishment of two free ports, one at each end of the said canal.

ARTICLE V.

The contracting parties further engage that, when the said canal shall have been completed, they will protect it from interruption, seizure, or unjust confiscation, and that they will guarantee the neutrality thereof, so that the said canal for ever will be open and free, and the capital invested therein, secure. Nevertheless the governments of the United States and Great Britain, in according their protection to the construction of the said canal, and guaranteeing its neutrality and security when completed, always understand that this protection and guarantee are granted conditionally, and may be withdrawn by both governments, or either government, if both governments, or either government, should deem that the persons or company undertaking or managing the same adopt or establish such regulations concerning the traffic thereupon as are contrary to the spirit and intention of this convention, either by making unfair discriminations in favour of the commerce of one of the contracting parties over the commerce of the other, or by imposing oppressive exactions or unreasonable tolls upon passengers, vessels, goods, wares, merchandise, or other articles. Neither party, however, shall withdraw the aforesaid protection and guarantee without first giving six months' notice to the other.

ARTICLE VI.

The contracting parties in this convention engage to invite every state with which both or either have friendly intercourse, to enter into stipulations with them similar to those which they have entered into with each other; to the end that all other states may share in the honour and advantage of having contributed to a work of such general interest and importance as the canal herein contemplated. And the contracting parties likewise agree, that each shall enter into treaty stipulations with such of the Central American States as they may deem advisable, for the purpose of more effectively carrying out the great design of this convention, namely, that of constructing and maintaining the said canal as a ship communication between the two oceans for the benefit of mankind, on equal terms to all, and of protecting the same; and they also agree that the good offices of either shall be employed, when requested by the other, in aiding and assisting the negotiation of such treaty stipulations; and should any difference arise as to the right or property through which the said canal shall pass between the states or governments of Central America, and such differences should in any way impede or obstruct the execution of the said canal, the governments of the United States and Great Britain will use their good offices to settle such differences in a manner best suited to promote the interests of the said canal, and to strengthen the bonds of friendship and alliance that exist between the contracting parties.

ARTICLE VII.

It being desirable that no time should be unnecessarily lost in commencing and constructing the said canal, the governments of the United States and Great Britain determine to give their support and encouragement to such persons or company as may first offer to commence the same, with the necessary capital, the consent of the local authorities, and on such principles as accord with the spirit and intention of this convention; and if any person or company should already have, with any state through which the proposed ship canal may pass, a contract for the construction of such a canal as that specified in this convention, to the stipulations of which contract neither of the contracting parties in this convention have any just cause to object; and the said persons or company shall, moreover, have made preparations, and expended time, money, or trouble on the faith of such contract, it is hereby agreed that such persons or company shall have a priority of claim over every other person, persons, or company, to the protection of the governments of the United States and Great Britain, and be allowed a year, from the date of the exchange of the ratifications of this convention, for concluding their arrangements, and presenting evidence of sufficient capital subscribed to accomplish the contemplated undertaking; it being understood that if, at the expiration of the aforesaid period, such persons or company be not able to commence and carry out the proposed enterprise, then the governments of the United States and Great Britain shall be free to afford their protection to any other persons or company that shall be prepared to commence and proceed with the construction of the canal in question.

ARTICLE VIII.

The governments of the United States and Great Britain having not only desired, in entering into this convention, to accomplish a particular object, but also to establish a general principle, they hereby agree to extend their protection, by treaty stipulations, to any other practicable communications, whether by canal or railway, across the isthmus which connects North and South America; and especially to the interoceanic communications, should the same prove to be practicable, whether by canal or railway, which are now proposed to be established by way of Tehuantepec or Panama. In granting, however, their joint protection to any such canals or railways as are by this article specified, it is always understood by the United States and Great Britain that the parties constructing or owning the same shall impose no other charges or conditions of traffic thereupon than the aforesaid governments shall approve of as just and equitable; and that the said canals or railways, being open to the citizens or subjects of the United States and Great Britain on equal terms, shall also be open on like terms to the citizens and subjects of every other state which is willing to grant thereto such protection as the United States and Great Britain engage to afford.

ARTICLE IX.

The ratifications of this convention shall be exchanged at Washington within six months from this day, or sooner if possible.

In faith thereof, we, the respective plenipotentiaries, have signed this convention, and have hereunto affixed our seals.

Done at Washington, the nineteenth day of April, Anno Domini one thousand eight hundred and fifty.

John M. Clayton.   (L.S.)
Henry Lytton Bulwer.   (L.S.)

APPENDIX III.

CONVENTION RESPECTING THE FREE NAVIGATION OF THE SUEZ MARITIME CANAL.

Signed at Cons ntinople, October 29, 1888.

IN the Name of the Almighty God, Her Majesty the Queen of the United Kingdom of Great Britain and Ireland, Empress of India; His Majesty the Emperor of Germany, King of Prussia; His Majesty the Emperor of Austria, King of Bohemia, etc., and Apostolic King of Hungary; His Majesty the King of Spain, and in his name the Queen Regent of the Kingdom; the President of the French Republic; His Majesty the King of Italy; His Majesty the King of the Netherlands, Grand Duke of Luxemburg, etc.; His Majesty the Emperor of All the Russias; and His Majesty the Emperor of the Ottomans; wishing to establish, by a Conventional Act, a definite system destined to guarantee at all times, and for all the Powers, the free use of the Suez Maritime Canal, and thus to complete the system under which the navigation of this canal has been placed by the Firman of His Imperial Majesty the Sultan, dated the 22nd February, 1866 (2 Zilkádé, 1282), and sanctioning the concessions of His Highness the Khedive, have named as their Plenipotentiaries, that is to say :—

(Here follow the names.)

Who, having communicated to each other their respective full powers, found in due and good form, have agreed upon the following articles :—

ARTICLE I.

The Suez Maritime Canal shall always be free and open, in time of war as in time of peace, to every vessel of commerce or of war, without distinction of flag.

Consequently, the high contracting parties agree not in

any way to interfere with the free use of the canal, in time of war as in time of peace.

The canal shall never be subjected to the exercise of the right of blockade.

ARTICLE II.

The high contracting parties, recognising that the Fresh-Water Canal is indispensable to the Maritime Canal, take note of the engagements of His Highness the Khedive towards the Universal Suez Canal Company as regards the Fresh-Water Canal; which engagements are stipulated in a convention bearing date the 18th March 1863, containing an *exposé* and four articles.

They undertake not to interfere in any way with the security of that canal and its branches, the working of which shall not be exposed to any attempt at obstruction.

ARTICLE III.

The high contracting parties likewise undertake to respect the plant, establishments, buildings, and works of the Maritime Canal and of the Fresh-Water Canal.

ARTICLE IV.

The Maritime Canal remaining open in time of war as a free passage, even to the ships of war of belligerents, according to the terms of Article I. of the present treaty, the high contracting parties agree that no right of war, no act of hostility nor any act having for its object to obstruct the free navigation of the canal, shall be committed in the canal and its ports of access, as well as within a radius of three marine miles from those ports, even though the Ottoman Empire should be one of the belligerent powers.

Vessels of war of belligerents shall not revictual or take in stores in the canal and its ports of access, except in so far as they may be strictly necessary. The transit of the aforesaid vessels through the canal shall be effected with the least possible delay, in accordance with the regulations in force, and without any other intermission than that resulting from the necessities of the service.

Their stay at Port Said and in the roadstead of Suez shall not exceed twenty-four hours, except in case of distress. In such case they shall be bound to leave as soon as possible. An interval of twenty-four hours shall always elapse between the sailing of a belligerent ship from one of the ports of access and the departure of a ship belonging to the hostile power.

ARTICLE V.

In time of war belligerent powers shall not disembark nor embark within the canal and its ports of access, either troops, munitions, or materials of war. But in case of an accidental hindrance in the canal men may be embarked or disembarked at the ports of access by detachments not exceeding 1000 men, with a corresponding amount of war material.

ARTICLE VI.

Prizes shall be subjected, in all respects, to the same rules as vessels of war of belligerents.

ARTICLE VII.

The powers shall not keep any vessel of war in the waters of the canal (including Lake Timsah and the Bitter Lakes). Nevertheless they may station vessels of war in the ports of access of Port Said and Suez, the number of which shall not exceed two for each power.

This right shall not be exercised by belligerents.

ARTICLE VIII.

The agents in Egypt of the signatory powers of the present treaty shall be charged to watch over its execution. In case of any event threatening the security or the free passage of the canal, they shall meet on the summons of three of their number under the presidency of their Doyen, in order to proceed to the necessary verifications. They shall inform the Khedival government of the danger which they may have perceived, in order that that government may take proper steps to ensure the protection and the free use of the canal. Under any circumstances, they shall meet once a year to take note of the execution of the treaty.

The last-mentioned meetings shall take place under the presidency of a special commissioner nominated for that purpose by the Imperial Ottoman government. A commissioner of the Khedive may also take part in the meeting, and may preside over it in case of absence of the Ottoman commissioner.

They shall especially demand the suppression of any work or dispersion of any assemblage on either bank of the canal, the object or effect of which might be to interfere with the liberty and the entire security of the navigation.

ARTICLE IX.

The Egyptian government shall, within the limits of the powers resulting from the Firmans, and under the conditions provided for in the present treaty, take the necessary measures for ensuring the execution of the said treaty.

In case the Egyptian government should not have sufficient means at its disposal, it shall call upon the Imperial Ottoman government, which shall take the necessary measures to respond to such appeal; shall give notice thereof to the signatory powers of the Declaration of London of the 17th of March, 1885; and shall, if necessary, concert with them on the subject.

The provisions of Articles IV., V., VII., and VIII. shall not interfere with the measures which shall be taken in virtue of the present article.

ARTICLE X.

Similarly the provisions of Articles IV., V., VII., and VIII. shall not interfere with the measures which His Majesty the Sultan and His Majesty the Khedive, in the name of His Imperial Majesty, and within the limits of the Firmans granted, might find it necessary to take for securing by their own forces the defence of Egypt and the maintenance of public order.

In case His Imperial Majesty the Sultan, or His Highness the Khedive, should find it necessary to avail themselves of the exceptions for which this article provides, the signatory powers of the Declaration of London shall be notified thereof by the Imperial Ottoman government.

It is likewise understood that the provisions of the four articles aforesaid shall in no case occasion any obstacle to the measures which the Imperial Ottoman government may think it necessary to take in order to ensure by its own forces the defence of its other possessions situated on the eastern coast of the Red Sea.

ARTICLE XI.

The measures which shall be taken in the cases provided for by Articles IX. and X. of the present treaty shall not interfere with the free use of the canal. In the same cases, the erection of permanent fortifications contrary to the provisions of Article VIII. is prohibited.

ARTICLE XII.

The high contracting parties, by application of the principle of equality as regards the free use of the canal, a principle which forms one of the bases of the present treaty, agree that none of them shall endeavour to obtain with respect to the canal territorial or commercial advantages or privileges in any international arrangements which may be concluded. Moreover, the rights of Turkey as the territorial power are reserved.

ARTICLE XIII.

With the exceptions of the obligations expressly provided by the clauses of the present treaty, the sovereign rights of His Imperial Majesty the Sultan, and the rights and immunities of His Highness the Khedive, resulting from the Firmans, are in no way affected.

ARTICLE XIV.

The high contracting parties agree that the engagements resulting from the present treaty shall not be limited by the duration of the acts of concession of the Universal Suez Canal Company.

ARTICLE XV.

The stipulations of the present treaty shall not interfere with the sanitary measures in Egypt.

ARTICLE XVI.

The high contracting parties agree to bring the present treaty to the knowledge of the states which have not signed it, inviting them to accede to it.

ARTICLE XVII.

The present treaty shall be ratified, and the ratifications shall be exchanged at Constantinople within the space of one month, or sooner if possible.

In faith of which the respective plenipotentiaries have signed the present treaty, and have affixed to it the seals of their arms.

Done at Constantinople, the 29th day of the month of October, in the year 1888.

For Great Britain .	(L.S.)	W. A. WHITE.
„ Germany . .	(L.S.)	RADOWITZ.
„ Austria-Hungary	(L.S.)	CALICE.
„ Spain . . .	(L.S.)	MANUEL FLOREZ Y GARCÍA.
„ France . .	(L.S.)	G. DE MONTEBELLO.
„ Italy . . .	(L.S.)	A. BLANC.
„ Netherlands .	(L.S.)	GUS. KEUN.
„ Russia . .	(L.S.)	NÉLIDOW.
„ Turkey . .	(L.S.)	M. SAÏD.

APPENDIX IV.

TREATY BETWEEN GREAT BRITAIN AND THE
UNITED STATES TO FACILITATE THE CON-
STRUCTION OF A SHIP CANAL (HAY-PAUNCE-
FOTE TREATY).

Concluded November 18, 1901.

THE United States of America, and His Majesty Edward
the Seventh, of the United Kingdom of Great Britain and
Ireland, and of the British Dominions beyond the Seas,
King, and Emperor of India, being desirous to facilitate the
construction of a ship canal to connect the Atlantic and
the Pacific Oceans, by whatever route may be considered
expedient, and to that end to remove any objection which
may arise out of the Convention of the 19th April, 1850,
commonly called the *Clayton-Bulwer Treaty*, to the construction of such canal under the auspices of the Government of the United States, without impairing the "general
principle" of neutralisation established in Article VIII. of
that Convention, have for that purpose appointed as their
Plenipotentiaries:—

The President of the United States, John Hay, Secretary
of State of the United States of America ;

And His Majesty Edward the Seventh, of the United
Kingdom of Great Britain and Ireland, and of the British
Dominions beyond the Seas, King, and Emperor of India,
the Right Honourable Lord Pauncefote, G.C.B., G.C.M.G.,
His Majesty's Ambassador Extraordinary and Pleni-
potentiary to the United States ;

Who, having communicated to each other their full
powers, which were found to be in due and proper form,
have agreed upon the following articles:—

ARTICLE I.

The high contracting parties agree that the present treaty shall supersede the afore-mentioned convention of the 19th April, 1850.

ARTICLE II.

It is agreed that the canal may be constructed under the auspices of the government of the United States, either directly at its own cost, or by gift or loan of money to indivividuals or corporations, or through subscription to or purchase of stock and shares, and that, subject to the provisions of the present treaty, the said government shall have and enjoy all the rights incident to such construction, as well as the exclusive right of providing for the regulation and management of the canal.

ARTICLE III.

The United States adopts, as the basis of the neutralisation of such ship canal, the following rules, substantially embodied in the convention of Constantinople, signed the 29th of October, 1888, for the free navigation of the Suez Canal, that is to say:—

1. The canal shall be free and open to the vessels of commerce and of war of all nations observing these rules, on terms of entire equality, so that there shall be no discrimination against any such nation, or its citizens or subjects, in respect of the conditions of the charges of traffic, or otherwise. Such conditions and charges of traffic shall be just and equitable.

2. The canal shall never be blockaded, nor shall any right of war be exercised nor any act of hostility be committed within it. The United States, however, shall be at liberty to maintain such military police along the canal as may be necessary to protect it against lawlessness and disorder.

3. Vessels of war of a belligerent shall not revictual nor take any stores in the canal except so far as may be strictly necessary; and the transit of such vessels through the canal shall be effected with the least possible delay in accordance with the regulations in force, and with only such intermission as may result from the necessities of the service.

Prizes shall be in all respects subject to the same rules as vessels of war of the belligerents.

4. No belligerent shall embark or disembark troops, munitions of war, or warlike materials in the canal, except in case of accidental hindrance of the transit, and in such case the transit shall be resumed with all possible dispatch.

5. The provisions of this article shall apply to waters adjacent to the canal, within three marine miles at either end. Vessels of war of a belligerent shall not remain in such waters longer than twenty-four hours at any one time, except in case of distress, and in such case shall depart as soon as possible; but a vessel of war of one belligerent shall not depart within twenty-four hours from the departure of a vessel of war of the other belligerent.

6. The plant, establishments, buildings, and all work necessary to the construction, maintenance, and operation of the canal shall be deemed to be part thereof, for the purposes of this treaty, and in time of war, as in time of peace, shall enjoy complete immunity from attack or injury by belligerents, and from acts calculated to impair their usefulness as part of the canal.

ARTICLE IV.

It is agreed that no change of territorial sovereignty or of the international relations of the country or countries traversed by the before-mentioned canal shall affect the general principle of neutralisation or the obligation of the high contracting parties under the present treaty.

ARTICLE V.

The present treaty shall be ratified by the President of the United States, by and with the consent of the Senate thereof, and by His Britannic Majesty; and the ratifications shall be exchanged at Washington or at London at the earliest possible time within six months from the date hereof.

In faith whereof the respective plenipotentiaries have signed this treaty and thereunto affixed their seals.

Done in duplicate at Washington, the 18th day of November, in the year of our Lord one thousand nine hundred and one.

JOHN HAY. (Seal)
PAUNCEFOTE. (Seal)

APPENDIX V.

CONVENTION BETWEEN THE UNITED STATES AND
THE REPUBLIC OF PANAMA FOR THE CON-
STRUCTION OF A SHIP CANAL TO CONNECT
THE WATERS OF THE ATLANTIC AND PACIFIC
OCEANS.

Signed at Washington, November 18, 1903.

THE United States of America and the Republic of Panama
being desirous to insure the construction of a ship canal
across the Isthmus of Panama to connect the Atlantic and
Pacific Oceans, and the Congress of the United States of
America having passed an Act approved June 28, 1902, in
furtherance of that object, by which the President of the
United States is authorised to acquire within a reasonable
time the control of the necessary territory of the Republic
of Colombia, and the sovereignty of such territory being
actually vested in the Republic of Panama, the high contracting parties have resolved for that purpose to conclude a
convention and have accordingly appointed as their plenipotentiaries—

The President of the United States of America, John
Hay, Secretary of State; and

The Government of the Republic of Panama, Philippe
Bunau-Varilla, Envoy Extraordinary and Minister Plenipotentiary of the Republic of Panama, thereunto specially
empowered by said government, who after communicating
with each other their respective full powers, found to be in
good and due form, have agreed upon and concluded the
following articles:—

ARTICLE I.

The United States guarantees and will maintain the
independence of the Republic of Panama.

ARTICLE II.

The Republic of Panama grants to the United States in perpetuity the use, occupation, and control of a zone of land and land under water for the construction, maintenance, operation, sanitation, and protection of said canal, of the width of ten miles extending to the distance of five miles on each side of the centre line of the route of the canal to be constructed; the said zone beginning in the Caribbean Sea three marine miles from mean water mark, and extending to and across the Isthmus of Panama into the Pacific Ocean to a distance of three marine miles from mean low water mark, with the proviso that the cities of Panama and Colon and the harbours adjacent to said cities, which are included within the boundaries of the zone above described, shall not be included within this grant. The Republic of Panama further grants to the United States in perpetuity the use, occupation, and control of any other lands and waters outside of the zone above described which may be necessary and convenient for the construction, maintenance, sanitation, and protection of the said canal or of any auxiliary canals or other works necessary and convenient for the construction, maintenance, operation, and protection of the said enterprise.

The Republic of Panama further grants in like manner to the United States in perpetuity all islands within the limits of the zone above described and in addition thereto the group of small islands in the Bay of Panama, named Perico, Naos, Culebra, and Flamenco.

ARTICLE III.

The Republic of Panama grants to the United States all the rights, power and authority within the zone mentioned and described in Article II. of this agreement, and within the limits of all auxiliary lands and waters mentioned and described in said Article II. which the United States would possess and exercise if it were the sovereign of the territory within which said lands and waters are located, to the entire exclusion of the exercise by the Republic of Panama of any such sovereign rights, power and authority.

ARTICLE IV.

As rights subsidiary to the above grants, the Republic of Panama grants in perpetuity to the United States the right to use the rivers, streams, lakes, and other bodies of water within its limits for its navigation, the supply of water or water-power or other purposes, so far as the use of said rivers, streams, lakes, and bodies of water and the waters thereof may be necessary and convenient for the construction, maintenance, operation, sanitation, and protection of the said canal.

ARTICLE V.

The Republic of Panama grants to the United States in perpetuity a monopoly for the construction, maintenance, and operation of any system of communication by means of canal or railroad across its territory between the Caribbean Sea and the Pacific Ocean.

ARTICLE VI.

The grants herein contained shall in no manner invalidate the title rights of private land-holders or owners of private property in the said zone or in or to any of the lands or waters granted to the United States by the provisions of any article of this treaty, nor shall they interfere with the rights of way over the public roads passing through the said zone or over any of the said lands or waters unless said rights of way or private rights shall conflict with rights herein granted to the United States, in which case the rights of the United States shall be superior. All damages caused to the owners of private lands or private property of any kind by reason of the grants contained in this treaty or by reason of the operations of the United States, its agents or employees, or by reason of the construction, maintenance, operation, sanitation, and protection of the said canal or of the works of sanitation and protection herein provided for, shall be appraised and settled by a joint commission appointed by the governments of the United States and the Republic of Panama, whose decisions as to such damages shall be final, and whose awards as to damages shall be paid solely by the Unites States. No part of the works on said canal or the Panama railroad or any auxiliary works relating thereto and authorised by the terms of this treaty shall be prevented, delayed or impeded by or pending such proceedings to ascertain such damages. The appraisal of said private lands and private property and the assessment of damages to them shall be based upon their value before the date of this convention.

ARTICLE VII.

The Republic of Panama grants to the United States within the limits of the cities of Panama and Colon and their adjacent harbours, and within the territory adjacent thereto, the right to acquire by purchase or by the exercise of the right of eminent domain, any lands, buildings, water rights or other properties necessary and convenient for the construction, maintenance, operation, and protection of the canal and of any works of sanitation, such as the collection and disposition of sewage and the distribution of water in the said cities of Panama and Colon, which, in the discretion of the United States may be necessary and convenient for the construction, maintenance, operation, sanitation, and protection of the said canal and railroad. All such works of sanitation, collection and disposition of sewage and distribution of water in the cities of Panama and Colon, shall be made at the expense of the United States, and the government of the United States, its agents or nominees, shall be authorised to impose and collect water rates, sewage rates which shall be sufficient to provide for the payment of interest and the amortisation of the principal of the cost of said works within a period of fifty years, and upon the expiration of said term of fifty years the system of sewers and water works shall revert to and become the properties of the cities of Panama and Colon respectively, and the use of the water shall be free to the inhabitants of Panama and Colon, except to the extent that water rates may be necessary for the operation and maintenance of said system of sewers and water.

The Republic of Panama agrees that the cities of Panama and Colon shall comply in perpetuity with the sanitary ordinances whether of a preventive or curative character prescribed by the United States and in case the government of Panama is unable or fails in its duty to enforce this compliance by the cities of Panama and Colon with the sanitary ordinances of the United States, the Republic of Panama grants to the United States the right and authority to enforce the same.

The same right and authority are granted to the United States for the maintenance of public order in the cities of Panama and Colon and the territories and harbours adjacent thereto in case the Republic of Panama should not be, in the judgment of the United States, able to maintain such order.

Article VIII.

The Republic of Panama grants to the United States all rights which it now has or hereafter may acquire to the property of the New Panama Canal Company as a result of the transfer of sovereignty from the Republic of Colombia to the Republic of Panama over the Isthmus of Panama, and authorises the New Panama Canal Company to sell and transfer to the United States its rights, privileges, properties, and concessions as well as the Panama Railroad and all the shares or part of the shares of that company; but the public lands situated outside of the zone described in Article II. of this treaty now included in the concessions to both said enterprises, and not required in the construction or operation of the canal shall revert to the Republic of Panama, except any property now owned by or in the possession of the said companies within Panama or Colon or the ports or terminals thereof.

Article IX.

The United States agrees that the ports at either entrance of the canal and the waters thereof, and the Republic of Panama agrees that the towns of Panama and Colon shall be free for all time, so that there shall not be imposed or collected custom-house tolls, tonnage, anchorage, lighthouse, wharf, pilot, or quarantine dues, or any other charges or taxes of any kind upon any vessel using or passing through the canal or belonging to or employed by the United States, directly or indirectly, in connection with the construction, maintenance, operation, sanitation, and protection of the main canal, or auxiliary works, or upon the cargo, officers, crew, or passengers of any such vessels, except any such tolls and charges as may be imposed by the United States for the use of the canal and other works, and except tolls and charges imposed by the Republic of Panama upon merchandise destined to be introduced for the consumption of the rest of the Republic, and upon vessels touching at the ports of Colon and Panama and which do not cross the canal.

The government of the Republic of Panama shall have the right to establish in such ports and in the towns of Panama and Colon such houses and guards, as it may deem necessary to collect duties on importation destined to other portions of Panama and to prevent contraband trade. The United States shall have the right to make use of the towns and harbours of Panama and Colon as places of anchorage, and for making repairs, for loading, unloading, depositing, or transhipping cargoes either in transit or destined for the service of the canal and for other works pertaining to the canal.

ARTICLE X.

The Republic of Panama agrees that there shall not be imposed any taxes, national, municipal, departmental, or of any other class, upon the canal, the railways and auxiliary works, tugs and other vessels employed in the service of the canal, storehouses, workshops, offices, quarters for labourers, factories of all kinds, warehouses, wharves, machinery and other works, property, and effects appertaining to the canal or railroad and auxiliary works, or their officers or employees, situated within the cities of Panama and Colon, and that there shall not be imposed contributions or charges of a personal character of any kind upon officers, employees, labourers, and other individuals in the service of the canal and railroad and auxiliary works.

ARTICLE XI.

The United States agree that the official dispatches of the government of the Republic of Panama shall be transmitted over any telegraph and telephone lines established for canal purposes and used for public and private business, at rates not higher than those required from officials in the service of the United States.

ARTICLE XII.

The government of the Republic of Panama shall permit the immigration and free access to the lands and workshops of the canal and its auxiliary works, of all employees and workmen of whatever nationality under contract to work upon or seeking employment upon, or in anywise connected with the said canal and its auxiliary works, with their respective families, and all such persons shall be free and exempt from the military service of the Republic of Panama.

Article XIII.

The United States may import at any time into the said zone and auxiliary lands, free of custom duties, imposts, taxes, or other charges, and without any restrictions, any and all vessels, dredges, engines, cars, machinery, tools, explosives, materials, supplies, and other articles necessary and convenient in the construction, maintenance, operation, sanitation, and protection of the canal and auxiliary works, and all provisions, medicines, clothing, supplies, and other things necessary and convenient for the officers, employees, workmen, and labourers in the service and employ of the United States and for their families. If any such articles are disposed of for use outside of the zone and auxiliary lands granted to the United States and within the territory of the Republic, they shall be subject to the same import or other duties as like articles imported under the laws of the Republic of Panama.

Article XIV.

As the price or compensation for the rights, powers, and privileges granted in this convention by the Republic of Panama to the United States, the government of the United States agrees to pay to the Republic of Panama the sum of ten million dollars ($10,000,000) in gold coin of the United States on the exchange of the ratification of this convention, and also an annual payment during the life of this convention of two hundred and fifty thousand dollars ($250,000) in like gold coin, beginning nine years after the date aforesaid.

The provisions of this article shall be in addition to all other benefits assured to the Republic of Panama under this convention.

But no delay or difference of opinion under this article or any other provisions of this treaty shall affect or interrupt the full operation and effect of this convention in all other respects.

Article XV.

The joint commission referred to in Article VI. shall be established as follows :—

The President of the United States shall nominate two persons and the President of the Republic of Panama shall nominate two persons, and they shall proceed to a decision; but in case of disagreement of the commission (by reason of their being equally divided in conclusion) an umpire shall be appointed by the two governments, who shall render the decision. In the event of the death, absence or incapacity of a commissioner or umpire, or of his omitting, declining or ceasing to act, his place shall be filled by the appointment of another person in the manner above indicated. All decisions by the majority of the commission or by the umpire shall be final.

ARTICLE XVI.

The two governments shall make adequate provisions by future agreement for the pursuit, capture, imprisonment, detention, and delivery within said zone and auxiliary lands to the authorities of the Republic of Panama, of persons charged with the commitment of crimes, felonies, or misdemeanours without said zone, and for the pursuit, capture, imprisonment, detention, delivery without said zone to the authorities of the United States, of persons charged with the commitment of crimes, felonies, and misdemeanours within said zone and auxiliary lands.

ARTICLE XVII.

The Republic of Panama grants to the United States the use of all ports of the Republic open to commerce as places of refuge for any vessels employed in the canal enterprise, and for all vessels passing or bound to pass through the canal which may be in distress and be driven to seek refuge in said ports. Such vessels shall be exempt from anchorage and tonnage dues on the part of the Republic of Panama.

ARTICLE XVIII.

The canal, when constructed, and the entrances thereto shall be neutral in perpetuity, and shall be open upon the terms provided for by section 1 of Article III. of, and in conformity with all the stipulations of, the treaty entered into by the governments of the United States and Great Britain on November 18, 1901.

Article XIX.

The government of the Republic of Panama shall have the right to transport over the canal its vessels and its troops and munitions of war in such vessels at all times without paying charges of any kind. This exemption is to be extended to the auxiliary railway for the transportation of persons in the service of the Republic of Panama, or of the police force charged with the preservation of public order outside of said zone, as well as to their baggage, munitions of war, and supplies.

Article XX.

If by virtue of any existing treaty in relation to the territory of the Isthmus of Panama, whereof the obligation shall descend or be assumed by the Republic of Panama, there may be any privilege or concession in favour of the government or the citizens and subjects of a third power relative to an interoceanic means of communication which in any of its terms may be incompatible with the terms of the present convention, the Republic of Panama agrees to cancel or modify such treaty in due form, for which purpose it shall give to the third power the requisite notification within the term of four months from the date of the present convention, and in case the existing treaty contains no clause permitting its modification or annulment, the Republic of Panama agrees to procure its modification or annulment in such form that there shall not exist any conflict with the stipulations of the present convention.

Article XXI.

The rights and privileges granted by the Republic of Panama to the United States in the preceding articles are understood to be free of all anterior debts, liens, trusts, or liabilities or concessions or privileges to other governments, corporations, syndicates or individuals, and consequently, if there should arise any claims on account of the present concessions or privileges or otherwise, the claimants shall resort to the government of the Republic of Panama and not to the United States for any indemnity or compromise which may be required.

ARTICLE XXII.

The Republic of Panama renounces and grants to the United States the participation to which it might be entitled in the future earnings of the canal under Article XV. of the concessionary contract with Lucien N. B. Wyse now owned by the New Panama Canal Company and any and all other rights or claims of a pecuniary nature arising under or relating to said concessions, or arising under or relating to the concessions to the Panama Railroad Company or any extension or modification thereof; and it likewise renounces, confirms and grants to the United States, now and hereafter, all the rights and property reserved in the said concessions which otherwise would belong to Panama at or before the expiration of ninety-nine years of the concessions granted to or held by the above-mentioned party and companies, and all right, title and interest which it now has or may hereafter have, in and to the lands, canal, works, property, and rights held by the said companies under said concessions or otherwise, and acquired or to be acquired by the United States from or through the New Panama Canal Company, including any property and rights which might or may in the future either by lapse of time, forfeiture or otherwise, revert to the Republic of Panama under any contracts or concessions, with said Wyse, the Universal Panama Canal Company, the Panama Railroad Company, and the New Panama Canal Company.

The aforesaid rights and property shall be and are free and released from any present or reversionary interest in or claims of Panama and the title of the United States thereto upon consumation of the contemplated purchase by the United States from the New Panama Canal Company, shall be absolute, so far as concerns the Republic of Panama, excepting always the rights of the Republic specially secured under this treaty.

ARTICLE XXIII.

If it should become necessary at any time to employ armed forces for the safety and protection of the canal, or of the ships that make use of the same, or the railways and auxiliary works, the United States shall have the right, at all times and in its discretion, to use its police and its land

and naval forces or to establish fortifications for these purposes.

Article XXIV.

No change either in the government or in the laws and treaties of the Republic of Panama shall, without the consent of the United States, affect any right of the United States under the present convention, or under any treaty stipulations between the two countries that now exist touching the subject matter of this convention.

If the Republic of Panama shall hereafter enter as a constituent into any other government or into any union or confederation of states, so as to merge her sovereignty or independence in such government, union or confederation, the rights of the United States under this convention shall not be in any respect lessened or impaired.

Article XXV.

For the better performance of the engagements of this convention and to the end of the efficient protection of the canal and the preservation of its neutrality, the government of the Republic of Panama will sell or lease to the United States lands adequate and necessary for naval and coaling stations on the Pacific coast and on the western Caribbean coast of the Republic at certain points to be agreed upon with the President of the United States.

Article XXVI.

This convention when signed by the plenipotentiaries of the contracting parties shall be ratified by the respective governments and the ratifications shall be exchanged at Washington at the earliest date possible.

In faith whereof the respective plenipotentiaries have signed the present convention in duplicate and have hereunto affixed their respective seals.

Done at the city of Washington the 18th day of November in the year of our Lord nineteen hundred and three.

John Hay.   (Seal)
P. Bunau-Varilla. (Seal)

INDEX

ACTS OF HOSTILITY :
    not allowed in the canal, 112.
Adams, Mr. : United States Minister at London, 37.
Alaska :
    land and water near, claimed by Russia, 4, 72.
Amador Guerrero, Doctor Manuel : 65, 66.
Arbitration :
    refused by the United States for the solution of the Clayton-Bulwer difficulties, 32.
Argentine :
    in relation to the Straits of Magellan, 87, 92, 134.
Arthur, President : 49–50.
Australia :
    within more easy reach from the ports on the Atlantic coast of America, 103.
Ayon : See Dickinson-Ayon treaty.

BEAUPRÉ, MR. : United States Minister at Bogotá, 60, 61, 62, 64.
Belgium :
    is neutralised, 85, 135 ;
    keeps armies for purposes of defence, 132, 135.
Belize : 25.
Biddle, Mr. Charles :
    appointed to make investigations on the Isthmus, 14.
Bidlack, Mr. : American *Chargé d'affaires* at Bogotá, 17.
Black Sea : 87, 134.
Blaine, Mr., Secretary of State :
    on the policy of the United States with regard to the canal, 43 et seq., 75–6, 106 ;

Blaine, Mr.—*continued*
    on the Clayton-Bulwer Convention, 46–7, 75–6 ;
    on the neutrality of the canal, 45, 47.
Blockade :
    vessels using the canal shall not be subject to, 110, 111.
Boston, the : 66.
Buchanan, Mr. :
    on Great Britain's policy in Central America, 27 ;
    on the Clayton-Bulwer Convention, 32.
Bulwer, Sir Henry Lytton, British Minister at Washington :
    asked by Mr. Clayton to enter into negotiations, 29 ;
    concluded the Clayton-Bulwer Convention, 30.
Bunch, Mr. : British *Chargé d'affaires* at Bogotá, 39.
Buren, van, President : 14, 15.

CALIFORNIA :
    acquisition of by the United States and its effect on the isthmian transit, 15.
Canal Companies :
    See Canal Projects.
Canal projects :
    the Dutch scheme, 11 :
    discussed at the Congress of Panama, 10 ;
    by Nicaragua, 9, 13, 50, 53, 57 ;
    impetus on, 15 ;
    by Honduras, 36 ;
    by Tehuantepec, 15, 39 ;
    by Panama, 37, 39, 57 ;
    the French company, 39, 40, 41, 50, 53, 57.

STUDIES IN
ECONOMICS AND POLITICAL SCIENCE

A Series of Monographs by Lecturers and Students connected with the London School of Economics and Political Science.

EDITED BY THE

DIRECTOR OF THE LONDON SCHOOL OF ECONOMICS
AND POLITICAL SCIENCE.

---

1. **The History of Local Rates in England.** The substance of Five Lectures given at the School in November and December, 1896. By EDWIN CANNAN, M.A., LL.D. 1896; 140 pp. Crown 8vo, cloth, 2s. 6d. *P. S. King & Son.*

2. **Select Documents Illustrating the History of Trade Unionism.** I. THE TAILORING TRADE. By F. W. GALTON. With a Preface by SIDNEY WEBB, LL.B. 1896; 242 pp. Crown 8vo, cloth, 5s. *P. S. King & Son.*

3. **German Social Democracy.** Six Lectures delivered at the School in February and March, 1896. By the Hon. BERTRAND RUSSELL, B.A., late Fellow of Trinity College, Cambridge. With an Appendix on Social Democracy and the Woman Question in Germany. By ALYS RUSSELL, B.A. 1896; 204 pp. Crown 8vo, cloth, 3s. 6d. *P. S. King & Son.*

4. **The Referendum in Switzerland.** By M. SIMON DEPLOIGE, University of Louvain. With a Letter on the Referendum in Belgium by M. J. VAN DEN HEUVEL, Professor of International Law in the University of Louvain. Translated by C. P. TREVELYAN, M.A., Trinity College, Cambridge, and Edited with Notes, Introduction, Bibliography, and Appendices, by LILIAN TOMN (Mrs. Knowles), of Girton College, Cambridge, Research Student at the School. 1898; x and 334 pp. Crown 8vo, cloth, 7s. 6d. *P. S. King & Son.*

5. The Economic Policy of Colbert. By A. J. SARGENT, M.A, Senior Hulme Exhibitioner, Brasenose College, Oxford; and Whately Prizeman, 1897, Trinity College, Dublin. 1899; viii and 138 pp. Crown 8vo, cloth, 2s. 6d. *P. S. King & Son.*

6. Local Variations in Wages. (The Adam Smith Prize, Cambridge University, 1898.) By F. W. LAWRENCE, M.A., Fellow of Trinity College, Cambridge. 1899; viii and 90 pp. With Index and 18 Maps and Diagrams. Quarto, 11 in. by 8½ in., cloth, 8s. 6d.
Longmans, Green & Co.

7. The Receipt Roll of the Exchequer for Michaelmas Term of the Thirty-first Year of Henry II. (1185). A unique fragment transcribed and edited by the Class in Palæography and Diplomatic, under the supervision of the Lecturer, HUBERT HALL, F.S.A., of H.M. Public Record Office. With thirty-one Facsimile Plates in Collotype and Parallel Readings from the contemporary Pipe Roll. 1899; vii and 37 pp. Folio, 15½ in. by 11½ in., in green cloth; 5 Copies left. Apply to the Director of the London School of Economics.

8. Elements of Statistics. By ARTHUR L. BOWLEY, M.A., F.S.S., Cobden and Adam Smith Prizeman, Cambridge; Guy Silver Medallist of the Royal Statistical Society; Newmarch Lecturer, 1897-98. 500 pp. Demy 8vo, cloth, 40 Diagrams. 1901; *Third Edition,* 1907; viii and 336 pp. 10s. 6d. net.
P. S. King & Son.

9. The Place of Compensation in Temperance Reform. By C. P. SANGER, M.A., late Fellow of Trinity College, Cambridge; Barrister-at-Law. 1901; viii and 136 pp. Crown 8vo, cloth, 2s. 6d. net. *P. S. King & Son.*

10. A History of Factory Legislation. By B. L. HUTCHINS and A. HARRISON (Mrs. Spencer), B.A., D.Sc.(Econ.), London. With a Preface by SIDNEY WEBB, LL.B. 1903; New and Revised Edition, 1911, xvi; 298 pp. Demy 8vo, cloth. 6s. net. *P. S. King & Son.*

11. The Pipe Roll of the Exchequer of the See of Winchester for the Fourth Year of the Episcopate of Peter Des Roches (1207). Transcribed and Edited from the original Roll in the possession of the Ecclesiastical Commissioners by the Class in Palæography and Diplomatic, under the supervision of the Lecturer, HUBERT HALL, F.S.A., of H.M. Public Record Office. With a Frontispiece giving a Facsimile of the Roll. 1903; xlviii and 100 pp. Folio, 13½ in. by 8½ in., green cloth, 15s. net.
P. S. King & Son.

12. Self-Government in Canada and How it was Achieved: The Story of Lord Durham's Report. By F. BRADSHAW, B.A., D.Sc.(Econ.), London; Senior Hulme Exhibitioner, Brasenose College, Oxford. 1903; 414 pp. Demy 8vo, cloth, 3s. 6d. net. *P. S. King & Son.*

13. History of the Commercial and Financial Relations between England and Ireland from the Period of the Restoration. By ALICE EFFIE MURRAY (Mrs. Radice), D.Sc.(Econ.), former Student at Girton College, Cambridge; Research Student of the London School of Economics and Political Science. 1903; 486 pp. Demy 8vo, cloth, 3s. 6d. net. *P. S. King & Son.*

14. The English Peasantry and the Enclosure of Common Fields. By GILBERT SLATER, M.A., St. John's College, Cambridge; D.Sc.(Econ.), London. 1906; 337 pp. Demy 8vo, cloth, 10s. 6d. net. *Constable & Co.*

15. A History of the English Agricultural Labourer. By Dr. W. HASBACH, Professor of Economics in the University of Kiel. Translated from the Second Edition (1908), by RUTH KENYON (1908). Cloth, 7s. 6d. net. *P. S. King & Son.*

16. A Colonial Autocracy: New South Wales under Governor Macquarie, 1810-1821. By MARION PHILLIPS, B.A., Melbourne, D.Sc.(Econ.), London. 1909; xxiii and 336 pp. Demy 8vo, cloth, 10s. 6d. net. *P. S. King & Son.*

17. India and the Tariff Problem. By H. B. LEES SMITH, M.A., M.P. 1909; 120 pp. Crown 8vo, cloth, 3s. 6d. net. *Constable & Co.*

18. Practical Notes on the Management of Elections. Three Lectures delivered at the School in November 1909, by ELLIS T. POWELL, LL.B., B.Sc.(Econ.), Fellow of the Royal Historical and Royal Economic Societies, of the Inner Temple, Barrister-at-Law. 1909; 52 pp. 8vo, paper, 1s. 6d. net. *P. S. King & Son.*

19. The Political Development in Japan. By G. E. UYEHARA, B.A., Washington, D.Sc.(Econ.), London. 1910; xxiv and 296 pp. Demy 8vo, cloth, 8s. 6d. net. *Constable & Co.*

20. National and Local Finance. By J. WATSON GRICE, D.Sc.(Econ.), London. Preface by SIDNEY WEBB, LL.B. 1910; 428 pp. Demy 8vo, cloth, 10s. 6d. net. *P. S. King & Son.*

21. An Example of Communal Currency. Facts about the Guernsey Market-house. By J. Theodore Harris, B.A., with an Introduction by Sidney Webb, LL.B., London. 1911; xiv and 62 pp. Cloth, 1s. 6d. net; paper, 1s. net. *P. S. King & Son.*

22. Municipal Origins. A History of Private Bill Legislation. By F. H. Spencer, LL.B.; with a Preface by Sir Edward Clarke, K.C. *In the Press.* *Constable & Co.*

23. Some English Railway Problems. By Sir George S. Gibb. *In the Press.* *P. S. King & Son.*

24. Grants in Aid. A Criticism and a Proposal. By Sidney Webb, LL.B. *In the Press.* *Longmans, Green & Co.*

25. The Panama Canal: From the Point of View of International Law. By H. Arias, B.A., LL.B. *In the Press.* *P. S. King & Son.*

Series of Bibliographies by Students of the School.

1. A Bibliography of Unemployment and the Unemployed. By F. Isabel Taylor, B.Sc.(Econ.), London. Preface by Sidney Webb, LL.B. 1909; xix and 71 pp. Demy 8vo, cloth, 2s. net; paper, 1s. 6d. net. *P. S. King & Son.*

Series of Geographical Studies.

1. The Reigate Sheet of the One-inch Ordnance Survey. A Study in the Geography of the Surrey Hills. By Ellen Smith. Introduction by H. J. Mackinder, M.A., M.P. 1910; xix and 110 pp. 6 Maps, 23 Illustrations. Crown 8vo, cloth, 5s. net. *A. & C. Black.*

2. The Highlands of South-West Surrey. A Geographical Study in Sand and Clay. By E. C. Matthews. 1911. 5s. net. *A. & C. Black.*